Max Pemberton

The Sea Wolves

Max Pemberton

The Sea Wolves

ISBN/EAN: 9783744712224

Printed in Europe, USA, Canada, Australia, Japan

Cover: Foto ©Thomas Meinert / pixelio.de

More available books at **www.hansebooks.com**

THE
SEA WOLVES

To

MY FRIEND,

CLEMENT KING SHORTER,

I INSCRIBE THIS STORY WITH DEEP

REGARD.

AUTHOR'S NOTE.

IT may not be without interest here to recall the fact that tradition tells to-day of a woman in Southern Europe who takes with her to many cities the reputation of a wrecker. Nor is the scene of the work, which gossip ascribes to her, removed by many leagues from that shore upon which some of the happenings in this book are laid. The account of the means by which bullion is shipped to the Continent by two, at least, of our greater financial houses is, I believe, accurate in all its details. I am much indebted to one who has recently returned from Russia on such a business as I have here ventured to describe for many of the particulars incorporated in the story.

CONTENTS.

CHAPTER I.
The Witch-Finder 13

CHAPTER II.
The Recorder Intrudes 19

CHATPER III.
On Board the "Semiramis" 34

CHAPTER IV.
The Last Voyage of the Tug "Admiral" . . 46

CHAPTER V.
The Third Day After 69

CHAPTER VI.
Light—but not of Dawn 79

CHAPTER VII.
"A Tempest Dropping Fire" 85

CHAPTER VIII.
South for Corunna 93

CHAPTER IX.
The Tragedy of the Flight 100

CHAPTER X.
Into the Unknown Haven 113

CHAPTER XI.
On the Field of the After-Math 124

CHAPTER XII.
The First of the Spaniards 138

CHAPTER XIII.
The Cove of Branches 143

CHAPTER XIV.
To the Creek again 154

CHAPTER XV.
Kenner Agrees 161

CHAPTER XVI.
Gold from the Sea 168

CHAPTER XVII.
The Fight in the Cabin 177

CHAPTER XVIII.
Sea-Wolves at Work 192

CHAPTER XIX.
The Second Wrecking 204

CHAPTER XX.
The Man by the Door 213

CHAPTER XXI.
Flight to the Sea 221

Contents.

Chapter XXII.
The Hall of Fountains 235

Chapter XXIII.
A Warning in the Flesh 253

Chapter XXIV.
Beacons on the Heights 273

Chapter XXV.
The Second Peril of the Creek 280

Chapter XXVI.
A Strange Cry in the Hills 291

Chapter XXVII.
In the Valley of Silence 308

Chapter XXVIII.
The Harbour of the Pool 321

Chapter XXIX.
Matters of History 325

Chapter XXX.
The End of the Record 330

LIST OF ILLUSTRATIONS.

	PAGE
THE MOON FLOODING PICTURESQUELY UPON THE WILDNESS OF THE BAY . . . . *Frontispiece*	
"YE'RE BUSY UP THERE, BEDAD!" . *To face page*	54
UPON THEM THERE SHONE A GREAT LIGHT . ,, ,,	80
"SHOREWARDS IF YOU'D LIVE!" . . . ,, ,,	112
BURKE SHOT AT HIM TWICE . . . . ,, ,,	184
AT THIS HE CLUTCHED . . . . . ,, ,,	224
THE BODY OF BURKE THE SKIPPER WAS HANGING FROM THE LOWEST BRANCH . ,, ,,	258
"NOW—LET THEM SWIM!" . . . . ,, ,,	282
THE RAPIDS DROVE HER ONWARDS AT A HEADLONG PACE . . . . . ,, ,,	318

THE SEA-WOLVES.

CHAPTER I.

THE WITCH-FINDER.

"She's Spanish," said the American, Kenner; "you can put your bottom dollar on it—and look at her daughter."

The other man, a clean-shaven, long-faced, dark-haired Englishman, sitting before a well-chosen *déjeûner* on the terrace of the great hotel at Monaco. did not betray any desire to contradict the assertion.

"I've been looking at her daughter for half-an-hour," said he, "and if she'll be pleased to go on breakfasting, I'll make it an hour."

The American laughed cheerily with a great boyish laugh at the rejoinder, and took a cigar from a lizard-skin case.

"Wal," he remarked, "I've seen worse on canvas than the little girl with the straw hat and the streamers; but fix your eye on the maternal property, and I guess you'll shout glory! Why, man, she must be a hundred and four, and young at that."

"They made her out fifty in the smoking-room last night," remarked the other, "so she's got the benefit of the doubt, any way. It's a case of Beauty and the Beast, and both of them of the feminine gender. The proprietor here will spin yarns about the pair until you wink with listening. He kept me up on cheroots and bad whiskey until three this morning, and if I hadn't got a head like a warming-pan, I'd pass the tale on."

"Does he know where the old girl hoists her flag when she's at home?"

"Broadly—that is just enough to trouble the post-office. He says she's four walls and a precipice, which she calls a castle, somewhere in the north-west of Spain. Her profession, occupation, calling, or business, as they style it on the parish census, seems to be equally solitary—she's a wrecker, and she lives on the vitals of ships. What do you think of that?"

"I think he's a handsome liar."

"But he believes it; and he gave me a list as long as your arm of the properties she has acquired by what the policies call peril of the sea. Look at her now: she's eating oysters with her fingers, you'll observe, and swearing at the waiter in two languages. Isn't there a *prima facie* case for the assumption?"

The American, who, like the other, was a man of some thirty years of age, fell to stroking his wavy yellow moustache thoughtfully. He did not seem able to look away from the table, luxuriously shadowed by many palms, whereat the Spanish woman and her daughter were sitting. Of those, the mother demanded the more immediate notice. She was a woman gaunt and hag-like when your eyes fell upon her face, but of prodigious stature when she rose to walk, having the stride of a man and a gait which would have won applause upon a recreation ground. But age had worn furrows in the brown, hide-like skin of her ferocious countenance until nothing but her features was discernible at the first; and these, which once had given ornament to a remarkable face, now stood out upon it to disfigurement.

As for her daughter—the little Inez, they called her in the hotel—then eating fruit with youthful recklessness, while the woman at her side was breakfasting off oysters and champagne, she was the contrast which gave to the picture its relief of welcome light. Her hair was dark with the rich sheen of Southern strength; her eyes were black and vivacious; and her face was piquant and beautiful even after Northern traditions. Those who knew anything of her said that she was eighteen; and in this she had cheated the quick maturity of the land of Alcaldes and of garlic, for she did not look a day more, while her manner had all the childish unrest and the vivacity of an English boarding-school Miss. In truth, a stranger family never sought the hospitality of Monaco, or brought yacht over the unsurpassably blue waters of the tideless sea; and the interest of the American, Kenner, and of the listless Englishman, Arnold Messenger—commonly known as "The Prince"

—was entirely justified, even to the assumption that the crone-like woman had a past, and that her history was not to be told in the market-place.

Some of these thoughts were alive in Kenner's mind as he sat devouring his cigar and continuing to watch the woman and her daughter. The morning was glorious, for the sun danced with sparkling light upon the still Mediterranean, and shone from the white villas and the rocky promontory as it shines in the Riviera at the nod of spring, bearing full beams upon palm and aloe, and the glorious crannies of flowers which blossom with the salt spray upon them. Men in dazzling "blazers" moved in and out upon the terraces; the breeze of exulting freshness bore the strains of dreamy music upon its breath; a few yachts rode without motion under the shelter of the height of towers; tropic luxuriousness of Nature seemed to have pushed winter from her hold, and to have come with a rich store from the very heart of Africa. It was not a morning to think of gloom; but the immovable touch of depression suddenly held the American, and he could not shake it off.

"I tell you what, Prince," said he, breaking his chain of silence after many minutes, "if I sit here watching that hag eat oysters—she's had three dozen already—I shall go to sleep and dream she's sticking pins into my figger. She makes me think I've been out on Bad-Lands."

The Prince looked up in astonishment.

"You'd better turn witch-finder!" he exclaimed:

"the new Mat Hopkins and the crone of Monaco. I can see a deputation to put her through the water cure."

"You've the laugh of me right along, but that's not it. Did you ever know that I'd worked the second-sight trade, and made a hundred dollars a week in a barn-storming tour through the States?"

"You're clever enough," replied the other; "but I didn't know you'd ever done anything so honest."

"Wal, a man must have his recreation, and I took mine with mediums; you try it when you're down to a dime."

"That's about my point now, though I don't see what it's got to do with the woman and the oysters."

"Everything, Prince; and look here, I'm cleaned out if ever I had a clearer reading——"

"Of what?"

"Of the hag and of ourselves."

The Prince lighted a cigar, the smoke hiding the jeer upon his lips.

"Go on," said he.

Kenner gave his answer with great deliberation, but he wore the air of the most serious man alive.

"That's exactly what I'm going to do," he remarked; "and in five years' time you can remind me of what's been said. In the first place, I've met that woman before; in the second, I've got to meet her again; and at the next meeting she will best me or I shall best her; there'll be smart work, and lives lost."

B

The man was woefully earnest, and his eyes, shining with some excitement, were still fixed upon the crone of the table. But Messenger listened, and laughed aloud.

"Kenner," said he, "you'd have made a better comedian than ever you were table-turner. Don't you think you've fooled around enough?"

The answer was never given, for the Spanish woman had paid her bill and was leaving the terrace. In another hour she had quitted Monaco in her steam yacht, and nothing but the memory of a grotesque and singular personality remained behind her.

CHAPTER II.

THE RECORDER INTRUDES.

When Arnold Messenger gave me the bundle of papers from which in the more part this narrative of an episode has been put together, he forgot, at the same time, to present me with any facts in his past which would help the biographer of a very singular man to do him complete justice. I knew him in Monte Video as one who had played for a very great stake at no distant date, but had lost nigh all he had in the throw, even to the unquestioning friendship of the young man, by name Hal Fisher, who then accompanied him. Under such circumstances, the making of crooked paths straight and the removal of stumbling-blocks was a task which I could accomplish but partially, and with no measure of complete satisfaction. Of the man's youth or boyhood I could learn little, save that he had been sent down from Magdalen College at Cambridge, and had left the university without taking a degree. The after years of his coming to manhood seem to have been spent in indolent luxury; and even in exploits which, but for the financial advocacy of his uncle, a rich rubber factor in Grantham, would have led to his acquaintance with the criminal law. Such a fate passed him by, and that it failed to overwhelm him may be set down both to his remarkable, if misdirected, intelligence, and to this succour of which I have spoken.

During his wanderings in London two years after he left Cambridge, he had met the lad who, when I first encountered him, passed as his brother. The boy had befriended him in a street brawl, and mutual confidences being exchanged, a very strange and inexplicable intimacy had come about. Hal Fisher was the son of a coffee merchant in Liverpool. He had suffered much—his mother dying at his birth—from a brutal interpretation of paternal duty which his father expounded to him; and at the age of fourteen he had quitted the private school in Edgbaston, Birmingham, where the aforesaid apocalypse was developed fruitfully; and had come to the city as many have come, hoping, fearing, with no friends, no knowledge, no plan, no prospect. On the very evening of his arrival a chance curiosity led him to press into the heart of a crowd which had gathered —as British crowds will—to see one man set upon by five; and being led instinctively to the defence of the minority, he joined heartily in the fray, and found himself shortly after in the rooms of Arnold Messenger, where he told the grave, thoughtful, yet sympathetic stranger the whole history of his life.

The result was a friendship which endured unbroken for nearly forty months. Fisher had much learning for his years; he wrote a capital letter, he had read many books. And here you will note a strange freak of fortune, which placed so fine a lad in the company of one of the most plausible and most accomplished *chevaliers d'industrie* in London. Arnold Messenger at that time—and after, as I fear—got meat and drink only by unfailing trickery. He found it mighty convenient to use the powers of one who never questioned him, who gave him faithful service, who had no plaguing curiosity—above all, one who deemed him in some part a hero, and betrayed for him an ardent boyish affection. The man, who had never evinced a regard unto that time even for a dog, was led to reciprocate the attachment in a generous way. He found himself acting the part of an elder brother. He shielded the boy from any participation in his dangerous ventures; he had pride in the thought that Fisher believed him to be honest; and he spent his money for the lad's good with a generosity which proved that he had two sides to his character.

This, then, is the somewhat reserved and priestly-looking man whom I find a loiterer at Monaco, in the company of Kenner. His friend, the American, wore the reputation of riches, and had brought his yacht to the Mediterranean solely in search of pigeons to pluck, and schemes—honest or otherwise—to pursue. But fortune had not smiled either upon him or upon Messenger. They lost heavily at the tables, they were banned by the elect, they could not run down a single fool who would give heed to their multifarious schemes. For the Englishman the immediate future was so dark that he contemplated a thousand and one schemes by which he might delude trusting hotel-keepers, and quit Italy for a new campaign. Yet the spring of his knavish inspiration remained dry; the waters of roguery refused to flow.

This diminuendo of hope had just been struck when the pair encountered the Spanish woman and her daughter Inez. They watched her leave the town in her yacht, her ostensible destination being Genoa; after which they loitered for an hour about the quaint little harbour, and then returned, at Messenger's request, to hunt up the boys. Of these, I have spoken sufficiently of Fisher, now a lad of seventeen; but of the other, Sydney Capel, a young fellow of twenty-four, I learned but little. Fisher had met him at Monaco; in his account of himself, he said that he was a clerk in the firm of Capel, Martingale, and Co., the financiers, of Bishopsgate Street, his uncle being head of the house, and reckoned a man of much substance. He was quite a boy still in habit and achievement, and the lads rowed and sailed together every day, to their mutual satisfaction. When Messenger and the American found them on the morning I am writing of, they were in spurs and breeches, hot from a gallop, and already reducing the abundance of fish, flesh, and fowl which served them for *déjeûner*. And while they talked—which they did unceasingly—they never for a moment relaxed the grip of knife and fork, or gave the waiters a "stand-easy."

"I'll tell you what, Prince," said Fisher, attacking a dish of wild strawberries and cream with particular relish, "that road to Mentone is about the grandest bit I've yet done in explorations. I never saw anything like those carouba-trees in my life; and as for cypress and euphorbia, why, you can revel in them. We saw the Corsican snow caps again this morning—grand they were in the sun, just like the mountains in a 'Percy,' and as clear as a photograph—eh, Capel?"

Sydney Capel, who admitted with reluctance that beauty could be found four miles from Charing Cross, answered unpoetically, and with full mouth—

"Good old Corsica!"

"That's just where he's such a brute," continued Fisher, quite disregarding the animalism of the observation. "I show him a hill all alive with grey olives and lemon-trees, and he says that it reminds him of Regent's Park. I believe the only thing Capel cares for in the universe is a hansom cab or a theatre ticket."

"He's only chaffing you, Hal," said the Prince, who smoked with a pleasant smile as he listened to the babble; "if you treat him properly, he'll let you give him a whole essay on heliotrope, and a bookful of facts about the prickly pear."

"Will he?" replied Fisher, looking round for yet a further measure of sweet sustenance. "You don't know what an unartistic beggar it is—all facts and figures, like a calculating machine. What do you think now?—he's going back to London to-night to lug Heaven knows how many kegs of gold to St. Petersburg."

The American had been reading during this talk, but he looked up sharply at the words. The Prince, too, put down the paper he held in his hand.

"What's that?" he asked.

"Just what I want to know," continued Fisher. "I call it rot—why, it only seems yesterday that he came here."

"Must you really go, Capel?" inquired the Prince, with sudden interest.

"I'm afraid so; you see, twice every year our house sends some hundreds of thousands to St. Petersburg in the matter of the loan we got for Russia. My uncle likes me to be one of the two that look after the business, and so I'm going back."

"That's a queer job," remarked Kenner, with a delightfully assumed indifference. "How many of you round up the dollars, did you say?"

"Only two of us," said Capel, lighting a cigarette and lolling back to look away down the coast-line to Bordighera. "You see, there's no danger."

"Of course not," interrupted Messenger suddenly. "I suppose nobody ever knows when the money is going."

"Exactly—we have a special train from Fenchurch Street to Tilbury, a special cabin or tug from Tilbury to Flushing, and then we go right through to the Russian frontier."

"Do they give you a great time out yonder?" asked Kenner.

"By Jove! I should think they do; I was trotted all over St. Petersburg like a Grand Duke when I went there last winter—I never ate so much in a week that I can remember."

"So I should fancy," said Kenner, sinking suddenly back into his chair and taking up his book.

"By the way," said he, as if in after-thought, "I may skirmish awhile in your old city after this flower-show here—what's the number of your street, if I'm passing?"

"I've got Capel's address," interposed Fisher suddenly; "we're going to dine together when I get back."

"That's right," said the Prince, looking hard at Kenner as he spoke.

They did not question the lads further, nor even look at them, but had great occupation in the *causeries* of current French newspapers which lay about on chairs and tables in pictorial profusion. The contaminating example of silence seized upon the others—a musical silence, during which the leaves of the date-bearing palms swayed musically in the sea-breeze, and the melodies which Glück made floated up from terrace to terrace, to be lost in a crescendo of chatter and movement, or to mingle with the whispers of the wind to which the multi-coloured buds were opening. So full of seductive rest was all the environment of lake-like water and olive-capped hills, that to survey it in idleness, to draw deep breaths of intoxicating freshness, was sufficient pastime for the restless or the wanderer. Even the boys, given to mad desires to make this bill or that cape, to ensnare the unnameably poor fish of the Mediterranean, to do anything but vegetate, suffered it for a whole hour before the mood took them to round the Cap d'Ail and inspect the point of Villefranche. The idea was no sooner suggested by Fisher than Sydney Capel gave it an immediate imprimatur; and in the wealth of his self-satisfaction, cried, with one of the five Italian words he knew, "*Andiamo*! there's just time for an hour's spin, out and back. I say, Kenner, can we have your boat?"

"Why, certainly," said the American. "I guess the Prince and me don't hanker after sprat-fishing this watch—eh, Prince?"

"Don't consider me," replied the Prince quietly; "I'm going into the hotel to write letters."

"Then you'll want me?" cried Fisher dolefully.

"Not a bit of it. I've only got to tot down one or two things, and you're better out than in. We shall see you at dinner."

"Yes; Capel will have time to bolt something before he sets out on that money-grubbing business of his. We should be back by five."

They went off arm-in-arm towards the harbour, where the American's steam yacht *Semiramis* lay, and Fisher took the opportunity of the way to make a somewhat significant remark upon his friend and patron's scholarship.

"Poor old Messenger," said he; "I fancy him blundering through a dictionary without me. I never knew a man write such a fist or spell so badly in all my life."

"And yet they sent him down from the 'Varsity without a degree," interposed Capel, with malice.

"That's true; but he's the best chap alive, for all that. He's been more than a brother to me; and there's something else in the world besides spelling."

He always consoled himself with this reflection, which was the growth of an honest friendship; but upon this afternoon the Prince had scant need of his sympathy. He progressed without his amanuensis, to his satisfaction; for the truth was that he had no business of letter-writing at all. The moment the boys were out of hearing he had put his paper down, as Kenner had done: and the men, each desiring the other to begin, waited with a slight, but unusual, restraint upon them. This was but the restraint of an instant, neither boasting of any substantial mock modesty; and when once he spoke, the Prince had meaning in his voice.

"Kenner," said he, "I've a fancy to smoke a cigar out past the lower town. Are you that way?"

"I was going to suggest it," replied Kenner, with the frankest air possible; "let's get."

They moved from the terrace, and skirted round

the harbour to the Mentone Road, walking sedately, and without uttering a single observation until they had left the effervescence and the voices of those who served tables behind them, and were upon that perfect highway which is one of the continuing glories of the Riviera. There, but for a handful of loiterers coming from the olive-clad promontory of Cap Martin, they had no company; and the sun being almost in the zenith, they made yet a slower measure of progress. Again, as at the hotel, Messenger was the first to speak.

"Kenner," said he of a sudden, as he stopped and began to use his stick upon the hard road as a man uses a burin upon a block—"Kenner, that money could be acquired."

The American blew a great circle of smoke from his lips, and looked at the other full in the face.

"You've made an observation," said he, "which I've been looking for for the last ten minutes."

Messenger ceased to engrave unnecessary hieroglyphics upon the wayside when he had got the answer, and walked on briskly for a while, as a man whose active mind compels activity in his limbs. When he stopped again, it was at a fall of the road where the hedge was all ablaze with a burden of flower and fruit, and a little cascade of crystal water shot out a thousand lights, as of unnumbered jewels. There was a jutting out of the grass bank here which made a natural seat under a canopy of wisteria and laburnum, and the men went to it by a common impulse, and began to talk more freely.

"What I want to ask myself," said the Prince, resuming the broken conversation at the point he had left it—"what I want to ask myself is this: How comes it if these clerks—you can't call them anything else—are sent twice or three times a year to St. Petersburg with some tons of money, that none of our friends has ever had the mind to try his luck with them?"

"That's nat'ral," interrupted the American; "but who's going to say that they have heard of it? I've got a head pretty full of items, but this is a cablegram to me. You don't suppose the dude's people are going round to all the newspaper men with the tale: 'Here's five hundred thousand off to St. Petersburg again; come and have a straight talk about it.' They keep it under lock and key: that's their chart of safety, as any mule could see."

"I quite follow you," said Messenger, whose hair was streaming back from his forehead in the fresh breeze, and whose eyes shone queerly, as if reflecting the ardent thought of a keen mind behind them; "yet, when I really think of the matter, I can remember that I have heard the tale before. All these financial houses send bullion in big sums to the Continent at one time or other, and it's rare that they've any other guard than a couple of trusted clerks."

"And why should they?" asked Kenner, to whom reflection brought some disappointment; "why should they? Who could interfere with them? You've got to leave sticking up trains to our boys; it's played out in your country, I reckon. Even Red Rube himself wouldn't have taken it on, passage paid."

"All that's very true," said Messenger, "but it's premature. At the present moment I am putting a very simple question to myself. Let's suppose that a man of some intelligence came to hear that Capel, Martingale, and Co. were sending half-a-million to Russia, say in three months' time. We'll presume he's got money behind him, and is a man of big ventures. Naturally it would strike him that there's a weak spot in the arrangement somewhere, and that a clever hand, with time before him, should be able to lay it bare. I'd like to bet a hundred that I'd find it with five minutes' thought."

"Maybe," said Kenner, shaking his head as one who has no belief, "maybe; but I'd like to wager on the other thing. Not that you ain't smart, Prince— I don't know your fellow in the States—but it's just this: I don't believe there is any weak spot. Why, figure it out. They mail the money by a special car, by a special steamboat, and another special car. Where are you to scoop the Jack-pot if you've got a whole bank behind you?"

"The weak spot," said Messenger, with great deliberation, "is the tug. If the man that I have spoken of had the work in hand, he would make it his first business to square the skipper of the tug. After that, his course would be easy."

"How do you make that out? What could they do with a tug full of money between Harwich and the Scheldt? By gosh! you've the quickest head for bad conclusions that I've tapped yet. Don't you see that the packet would be cabled as missing to every port in the Channel, and stopped away this side of Ushant light? It's as plain to me as the hill-top yonder."

"Because you haven't brought any grip on it. The further I go into it the easier it seems. Let me give you the whole business in a few words. The man I have mentioned would, to begin with, leave this place to-night, and follow this Sydney Capel to London. There he would associate with him closely (taking rooms in his house, if possible) for the next three months. He would use what mind he had to the making of a friendship; and the leisure from this occupation would be given to the promotion of a good understanding (bought at any price) with the skipper of the tug who generally crosses with the money. It is no great strain to imagine that this man might find important business in St. Petersburg at the very moment when Sydney Capel next left with the bullion. For him to get a permit to go through by the special and the tug would be no unreasonable thing. I can imagine, too, that if he had a friend with a fast steam yacht, and if this friend met the tug by agreement in the North Sea, that the way would be clearer. Do you follow me thus far?"

"In a bee-line," replied the American, who smoked with a fury begotten of excitement.

"Well, we can see all the rest without a long bill on thought. The skipper of the tug has men to depend on aboard with him; the clerks, if they are not bought, get a couple of raps from a revolver-butt; the tug is scuttled, the money is shipped upon the yacht, and she steams north to reach the Atlantic. After that it's a mere pleasure trip."

He ceased to speak, the quick glow of interest passing from the face it had lighted as the sun passes from a cloud. But Kenner rose quickly from the grass bank, and with blanched face and dancing eyes cried—

"Prince, you're a genius, by thunder!"

"Do you think so?" asked Messenger. "But I was only giving a suppositional case. You'd want a cast-iron man to take the business on, and money behind him."

Kenner answered the suggestion with his customary and simple exclamation, "Let's get!"

The afternoon was passing, the west being already touched with that arc of deeper crimson which is the herald of twilight; and there were few wayfarers upon the road to Monaco. For some part of the way the men walked as they had come, in a meditative silence, but upon the threshold of the town the American stopped of a sudden, and asked his companion the abrupt question—

"Can you leave here to-night?"

Messenger displayed no shadow of surprise that it was put to him. He had been waiting for it since they had left the alcove of the orchids; and he answered it with another interrogation—

"If I could get five hundred and the promise of a couple of thousand in a month, I'd see my way."

"It's a big sum, Prince," urged Kenner laconically.

"And a big thing. I don't know that the figure isn't below the mark. Of course it would be share-and-share whatever's got as between man and man—and this money I want can go against the account when the time comes. You would bring the *Semiramis* to London directly I wire for you."

"That's fair sounding," replied Kenner, "and I don't know that I've got anything against it. I'll chew it in my mind for half-an-hour, any way."

"Take all the time you like," said the Prince; "to-morrow will do as well as to-day, though something might be got if a man followed this youngster to London to-night. By the way, if I go, you'll have Fisher with you for a couple of months' cruise—that's understood?"

"Why, certainly; but he'll be ashore later on?"

"Ashore—I fancy not. Would you be having him shout my history in the streets when my back's turned? If we go, he goes; that's as certain as the sun is sinking."

They entered the garden as they spoke, and went to Kenner's room. Two hours later Sydney Capel left for London; and Arnold Messenger, commonly known as "The Prince," went with him.

CHAPTER III.

ON BOARD THE "SEMIRAMIS."

At one bell in the first dog—the day being Wednesday, and the month July—the steam yacht *Semiramis* rounded the South Foreland, and dropped anchor amongst a fleet of wind-bound vessels which lay off the white town of Deal. She had taken a pilot from the Solent, for her skipper, Roger Burke, a huge man from San Francisco, knew nothing of English waters, and the main part of the crew was made up of niggers and of Lascars. She had for mate a slim, quiet man, named Parker; and her chief engineer was an Italian, whom she had picked up during a long cruise in the Adriatic. Yet she had been built in the Thames for the American, Jake Kenner; and in the matter of speed, or indeed of design, she had few equals amongst pleasure-boats. I have heard it said that she was one of the first yachts to be equipped with a tubulous boiler and with twin-screws; but her owner had gone to Thorneycroft's to buy one of the fastest vessels floating, and the firm had built for him a craft with all the rakish beauty of a cruiser combined with the speed and hull of a torpedo-catcher.

Not that she was by any means an enormous yacht, judging her by later-day standards. Her comparatively large engines allowed but restricted accommodation aft; and while her whole length was nearly two hundred feet, much of it was given to boilers and bunkers, and little to solid comfort. Yet she was a ship-shape-looking craft, with a crew of thirty men; and those on board had the satisfaction of knowing that she could hold her own with most things afloat if the need were that she should show her heels. Unhappily, I have nothing but a photograph of her to use in this account, for she was a wreck within a few weeks of the date when I first see her in my mind in the Downs; and of her idle, easy-going crew, but few lived to carry the remembrance of her.

The anchor being over, and the yacht riding easily upon a glassy sea, Roger Burke, the captain, came down from the spotlessly-white bridge, and descended the companion to the grey-and-gold saloon. He found Hal Fisher there, lying his length upon the velvet sofa, and absorbed in a heroic, if antique, story which dealt with the corsairs of Barbary. The lad looked up eagerly at his coming, and asked, unnecessarily, "Was that the anchor I heard them letting go?"

"Why, for sure; did you think it was the shooters or the coal?"

"Surly brute!" muttered the boy, as the colossal form of the skipper disappeared through the door which led to the private cabin; and he remembered that at last they must have come to the Downs. He had been following so closely the sufferings of five hundred Christians who had worked under the lashings of the Moors, that the whole business of bringing-to had escaped him. Yet he had longed for a sight of the white cliffs of England with that intense *nostalgie* which young travellers suffer. For three months he had not seen a wooded lane nor a really green field; for three months—and this was the sorer trial—he had not looked upon the one man who was as brother, father—indeed, the whole world of mankind to him. In the earlier days letters had been frequent; they had found them at Alexandria, at Cairo, and at Gibraltar, where for a few weeks prior to her voyage northward the yacht had been lying. But the Prince no longer wrote as once he had written in that terrible hand of his—boyish letters, full of gossip and good wishes—stunted and withered messages, half-promises, hints at business of exceeding importance, of such had been his communications at the end of it, until Hal began to ask himself, with no little dread, Is he tiring of me? Can I be of no more use to him? Has not the time come for us to take different roads in life?

He was not the one to suffer any mere charity. The moment he was sure that Arnold Messenger had wearied of him, he would make his own way, he declared. There were intervals when he was almost angry with the Prince for leaving him on

Kenner's yacht. How came it that he could not be in London with him?—of what sort were those affairs which could be manipulated by one who spelt "believe" without an "i," and put three "p's" in "proper"? The mystery was more than the lad's seventeen years of worldly knowledge could solve. He could only conclude, with a heavy heart, that the grip of evil fortune had clutched him once more, and that the road of life ahead of him lay through dark paths.

All this contributed to an inveterate longing to set foot in England. Had he but known what infinite perils awaited him on the shores of his own country his doubts and fears would have been of another mood. But suspicion was as far away from him as the poles, both at that time and until the more part of the evil was written. Indeed, when he came on deck to observe the white buildings and the conventional pier of Deal, with the hills and dales of lovely Kent, all fair and green in the ripe fulness of a generous summer, what gloominess he had passed from him, and gave place to an overwhelming gladness, because he knew that soon he would hear his one friend's voice again, and feel the grip of a hand which had done so much for him.

In this mood he stood upon the poop of the *Semiramis*, when Roger Burke, the skipper, went to the private cabin where Kenner sat. The two men were soon occupied in earnest conversation, the American having a long letter in cypher before him, as well as a telegram, with which he was more immediately concerned.

"Burke," said he, lowering his voice almost to a whisper, "this cablegram says, 'Stop in the Downs until I come.' Now, what does he mean by that? Here's the cypher; you can read it as well as I can —putting it plain that we were to be ready for the job by the eleventh of the month, and this is the tenth. What's the delay, and why?—unless he wants to fly the danger signal, and this is his flag."

The great skipper shook his head, and leant back on the sofa mystified.

"It's a job ez big ez oceans," said he, "and it's one chance in five hundred that he gets the leg of them. Don't you see that they may be on top of him long afore he's weathered London. By thunder! there ain't a man of us in it what hasn't got a rope round his gullet bought and paid for now, at the beginning of it—not a man of us."

Kenner was not convinced.

"You don't know the Prince," said he; "it's got to be a fire-and-blazes police to go one better than him, any way."

"I ain't contradictin' that," remarked Burke; "he may be as thick in grit as an out-West man, but he's a poor notion of showing it. What's he want this kid aboard for? let me ask. Is this a game of base-ball, or is it a job for men?"

"That's his business," replied Kenner, "and I guess it'll come out square when there's settling times. The question I've got to ask now is—Where's he laying for?—and when's the money going over?"

"That's it," said Burke, with a shrug; "and how many's got to share when the candy's split?"

Kenner had an answer upon his lips, but it stayed there, as a great sound of hailing was heard above and footsteps thudded upon the deck. In another moment the cabin-door opened, and Arnold Messenger entered. Though three months had passed since the American had seen him, his face was mobile and impassive as of yore, his manner as confident and easy, his self-possession as remarkable. He had a suit of blue-serge upon him that had come from a fine tailor, his brown boots shone like reflectors, his linen had an exquisite whiteness. And as he entered the cabin the others greeted him with a word of intense satisfaction and waited for him to speak, since the whole fortune of the enterprise hung upon his words.

"Kenner," said he, shutting the door behind him, and bolting it, "what I've got to tell must be told by the clock. I'll be wanting to reach London by the six fifty-five out of the town."

"You've half-an-hour," said Kenner laconically " Burke'll keep the gig out."

"That will suit me perfectly," replied the Prince, settling himself with provoking slowness at the table, upon which he laid some paper; "and if you'll get me ink we shall save talk."

Burke went to a cupboard at the request; but Kenner could not longer tolerate the mystery.

"Prince," said he, "out with it; is the money going, or do you throw the cards?"

"The money is going to-morrow night," answered Messenger, without moving a muscle of his face, "and the tug *Admiral* takes it from Tilbury to Flushing."

"Do you happen to know—that is, did you learn the amount?" asked the American, with a husky voice.

"One million sterling," answered the Prince, his face as placid as marble, and his nerves as steady as steel wires.

"By gosh!" said the American.

Messenger permitted to them a moment's silence in which to digest his words, and then continued with somewhat more satisfying detail—

"Kenner, there's been work to do since we parted, more than three months ago, which I never booked in my calculations the day this thing came to us at Monaco—you remember when. But that you've learnt of in my letters, and this is not the time to go into it. The first thing I've to ask you now is this— Have you got a man aboard here that you can't trust in the job, and if so, when are you going to send him ashore?"

Kenner did not answer the question himself, but turned to the skipper, Burke, who sat upon the edge of the bunk nursing his chin in his hand.

"Burke," said he, "that's your affair, I guess. What you don't know about them ain't worth the knowing."

The skipper raised his head at the appeal, and answered quietly—

"If I thought ez any of 'em was that way, I'd put bullets in 'em now, if you was to swing me afore two bells."

"That's all I wanted to hear," replied Messenger; "and in that matter I've no sort of doubt. The next thing to ask you is—How much are we going to tell them safely, and when are they to be told?"

"You've got to tell 'em a good deal, I reckon," said the skipper instantly: "a good deal, barrin' what your cargo's worth—the knowledge of that's between us three——"

"And the skipper of the tug," interposed Messenger; "a man among a thousand, he is— Kess Robinson by name, and as obstinate as a mule. I had to promise him twenty thousand pounds and a couple of thousand per man for his crew——"

"Are they all swore to it?" asked Burke sharply.

"Why should they be—now?" answered Messenger "Do we want them ladling it all over the town? But they're well chosen; and if there's to be trouble among them, it will come from the mate, Mike Brennan, a big honest fool, that I've talked to for a month, and made no more impression on than if he'd been cast-iron ballast."

"How many of 'em is to come aboard here?" asked

Kenner, somewhat anxiously. "You see, whatever they have, our lot's got to have the same, if they're going right along smooth with it."

"I've thought of that," replied Messenger; "put down forty thousand for the men together, and there needn't be a whisper; but you'll get all the arms you have aft, and if they've any pride forward, we'll have to begin the shooting."

"That's as plain as dough-nuts," cried Burke, snapping his fingers; "and it rests for us to know what our instructions is—you're mighty quiet about them."

"I am going to write them," said Messenger, taking up the pen and big sheet of foolscap, and speaking with an easy air of command, as one inheriting it—"I am going to make it so plain that a child of seven could follow it. In the first place, you will weigh the moment I am gone, and get into Sheerness for as much coal as you can carry, stacking decks as well as bunkers. You will lie at the river's mouth until to-morrow night—it may be until ten, it may be until eleven. The money will leave Bishopsgate Street somewhere about seven o'clock, and will be carried in a special train from Fenchurch Street to Tilbury, where it will be put, in charge of Sydney Capel and Arthur Conyers, the head clerk of the house, upon the tug *Admiral*. I shall be already upon the tug, which will weigh at once and proceed down river. At Sheerness we shall show a flare, when you, being ready to put out, will follow us as closely as common sense dictates, until we stand well in the North Sea, and clear of ships. We shall shape a course full N.E., to be out of the track of steamers, and when we are ready for you—which will not be until we have passed Hull—we shall send up a couple of rockets, and you will answer and make fast alongside, while we come over and bring the money. After that, as I said to you three months ago, it's a question of sea-legs."

The American listened to the clear enunciation of ideas with a close attention and admiration for the man whose brain could generate such a plausible hypothesis. There were yet, however, links missing from the chain as he saw it; and his first question was in a degree proof of his own shrewdness:

"These clerks, or whatever you call 'em," said he —"who's going to lay them out?"

"That depends on themselves, or on one of them, at any rate," answered Messenger, continuing to write. "You've read from my letters that Capel is in with us to his armpits. I bought him for a quarter share—as between you and me, Kenner—a month ago. He owes a matter of five thousand in London, and can't draw back—I've seen to that. He flew at the job almost before I'd opened my lips, and I'd trust him to the end of it. The other's a mere dummy, a numskull, who'll either cave in at the first show of fight or go under for his pains. It's the mate, as I said before, that's like to trouble us; the rest's a mere pleasure cruise."

"And the destination?" asked the American.

"Monte-Video first, and the blessed shades of the Argentine or Uruguay after."

He wrote out fully the directions he had given, marking the hours most plainly in uncouth if legible capitals; the others waiting for him patiently, though their excitement was palpitating and visible. When he had concluded the whole with a fine flourish, he looked at his watch, and said that he had ten minutes: a reflection which drew from the American the desire to "crack a bottle for luck."

"Which you'll need badly," muttered Burke. "I've no fancy for work begun on Fridays."

Messenger listened to him, a mocking sneer upon his lips.

"Burke," said he, "I've had fine accounts of you; and you're in for the biggest venture of your life. Are you going to play the old woman now?"

"By thunder! that's sense to the kernel," added Kenner. "We're afloat, and Heaven knows when we'll see the shore again——"

"That depends on us all," said Messenger, rising; "but if any man shows false, let him look to himself."

With this he went on deck, to find the gig waiting and Fisher leaning moodily upon the taffrail. For a moment he made as though to step into the boat without any notice of the lad; but a sudden impulse arrested him, and he took the boy's hand quickly, and spoke to him in a low voice:

"Hal," said he, "I've much to say to you, but this

is not the time. I shall be aboard here again in three days, and then I'll count upon you."

He was gone almost with his words; and while Fisher was yet thinking of them, the *Semiramis* had weighed anchor, and was standing in towards the river's mouth."

CHAPTER IV.

THE LAST VOYAGE OF THE TUG "ADMIRAL."

THE rain fell in torrents—pitiless summer rain, which the quivering ground swallowed greedily and the burnt and seared leaves drank up with unquenchable greed. For a month or more the consuming drought had settled heavily upon the city and the south, leaving to the intolerable sun the green of the earth and the fuller ripeness of the fields; but on that July afternoon the westerly gale had come to lave all things with its refreshing gifts, and to pour upon London that torrent-like draught which alone made life in her streets possible at such a season.

Towards evening the downpour, which had been gathering strength for some hours, burst with a new intensity, sweeping in rivers of water from the higher roofs, and swirling into dust-brown eddies at the choked grating of the sewers. The sky, which had presented a face of leaden cloud since mid-day, darkened almost as at the touch of night; the air seemed to exude an enervating heaviness; the wind swept from corner to corner, and from nook to nook, bending the younger plants like whips, and scattering the full blossoms from the gardens in showers of perfuming leaves. It was a night, verily, to shame summer: a night breeding thoughts of books and of the blessings of the lemon-tree and the cheapness of ice.

Sydney Capel, standing moodily at his window in the court of Danes Inn, arrived at these reflections, and at more, as the clock struck five, and an aged charwoman condescended to set his tea upon the table, and to make a delightfully vague remark—which served her for all weathers.

"Here's an everning agen," said she; and with that, she withdrew as quietly as she had come, and left her special charge to the last meal he would get before setting out on his long journey—ostensibly to the Russian frontier, in reality to some distant shore, of whose situation he was but vaguely conscious.

It has been said by those who saw Capel at this time that he was vastly changed from the man who had taken life so flippantly on the shores of the Mediterranean three months before. His face had lost its colour; his eyes were ringed about with purple hollows; he had a hacking cough, which rarely left him; he had lost much of his old spruceness in dress; he had become *blasé* and effeminate. Such a change was easy to account for by those who knew the inner pages of his life during those months when Messenger had wound the coils of his rope about him stealthily, until he held him on that day as a vaquero holds quarry in a lasso. It had been a quick fall; but the seeds which breed the tares of life had been in

Capel from his birth, and he proved plastic as clay in the hands of a man who moulded him with all the ready skill of an adventurer and a rogue. On that night the end had come, the parting of the ways—from a career, from friends, from his old world to the paths of danger, of darkness, and of doubt. Had it been possible, he would have turned back even then; but the web was too closely woven, the meshes of the net had ensnared him beyond hope.

A clock in the Strand struck the first quarter after five when he turned away from the sight of the relentless rain, and gathered his baggage together with a mechanical effort. He had prepared himself just that outfit which used to serve him on these trips when he took ingots across the Continent, and was fêted in St. Petersburg; but it seemed rather a mockery now to look upon a portmanteau with a dress-suit in it, or those other fripperies which were so purely ornamental. Nevertheless, they lay there in bulky confusion; and he went to work mechanically, waiting every moment to hear the sound of Messenger's steps upon the stairs and the knock upon his oak which was the very last he might expect to hear.

As the thing went, it was half-past five before the man appeared, a smile upon his face and an unusual colour in his cheeks. He was dressed in a short black jacket, with a white vest beneath, and carried no visible equipment save a light mackintosh for the long journey before him. But he spoke with an unusual rapidity of utterance, and could not check his uneasiness.

"Well," said he, the moment the door had shut behind him, "you're ready, I see."

"Yes," replied Capel coldly; "I wish to Heaven I were not!"

Messenger looked at him fiercely, but stopped the exclamation upon his lips, and said in a gentler voice—

"I've been young myself; I know the feeling, though I've lost it years since. Have a glass of brandy. Why, man, think of to-morrow."

"It's just what I'm thinking of," answered Capel: "to-morrow—and the years after."

Messenger laughed a little harshly, but said no more, and they went together to the Strand, where a cab was waiting for them. In ten minutes' time they were passing down Queen Victoria Street to the Bank; and at the doors of the latter they prepared to separate, the man going straight to Tilbury, Capel to the office of his firm, where he was to meet his fellow in the business, and to find the bullion. A very brisk *Au revoir* was all that came from Messenger's lips as he jumped from the cab to the pavement, but he turned again as Capel was closing the door, and said—

"Oh, by-the-bye, when we get aboard Kenner's yacht, you'll find young Fisher there. He knows nothing of this, of course, and we must make a tale before we meet him—he'll take any story you give him, as you know."

D

Capel looked up sharply at the intelligence, and asked—

"Is that all right? Don't you think there's a risk?"

The question was not answered, for the cab drove off at some pace down Lombard Street, and Messenger made his way quickly to the Tilbury and Southend Railway. At half-past seven he reached the dock station; five minutes later he was on board the tug *Admiral*. He found her aft-deck untenanted save by a great retriever dog, who had curled himself up near the trigger-hook; but three seamen in oil-skins were working at the moorings, and the skipper, Kess Robinson, a little, bullet-headed, red-haired man, who wore a kind of leather jerkin and a peaked cap, stood by them, swearing many strange oaths in many tongues. So occupied was he with his verbal fireworks that Messenger's coming escaped him for a moment; and when he did see him, he proved that he was in a very poor humour.

"You've come aboard, have you?" said he; "and time too, time too."

"What's wrong?" asked the Prince. "You don't seem exactly in a fête-and-gala temper. Is anything amiss?"

"Amiss enough," replied the fellow gruffly "This cursed warping's fouled, for one thing, and there's another—but I'll tell you aft."

In the small cabin or state-room, which serves the skipper's needs on a deep-sea tug, they sat down to have the few words possible before the final act in their laboriously-built drama began. Robinson closed the cabin door carefully after them, and went on to speak at once; while he helped himself to an elaborate potation from a bottle of Hollands gin.

"Fact is," said he, "this chap, our mate, Mike Brennan by name, doesn't go as easy to it as I should like. Not exactly that he scents we out, but he wants to know a long sight too much. He's ashore, and I'm looking for two of our new hands to soak him. If he comes aboard sober, there's wind to blow afore morning, as sure as we're sitting here."

"What about the others?" asked Messenger.

"There's six of 'em answering to their names, and three new. I booked 'em in the docks yesterday, and they're our sort. Then there's three old hands fit to work with me right through it, and the mate. But it's a swinging job, guvner."

The Prince lighted a big cigar and lay back on the cushions to think. He could not disguise from himself the fact that he had then embarked upon the greatest venture of his adventurous life, and even at the ultimate moment he could scarce believe that success could attend such a mighty *coup*. Yet he knew that he had given long nights to the framing of his plan; and if he alone had borne the responsibility, no second thought of its result would have come to him. But the burden was shared by many—it was impossible otherwise that the enterprise could have been set afoot—and the great *coup* once accomplished, the danger from babblers' tongues was indisputable. He knew well enough that success, full and unchecked, meant years of banishment to all of them; and while each man embarked had a stake big enough to make him hold his tongue, it was more than possible that failure might come—and then!

These reflections passed through his mind quickly as he heard Kess Robinson's tale; but whatever were his own qualms, he did not show them. Rather he maintained a bantering humour as he answered—

"Pooh, man! where's the trouble come in? This isn't the time to wear your heart on your sleeve. You're going to act now; and that reminds me—you've got a Colt on you?"

"Not me," said the skipper; "fire-irons ain't much in my line, and I don't see as we'll be wanting them."

"But this mate; what is to be done with him?"

"What the time and this handspike tell me."

More he did not say, for a seaman entered with the intelligence that the others had come; and the two men went on deck together with expectant haste. The tide was now full, and the rain had ceased—a glorious night following upon the tempest. From the docks of Tilbury the masts of many ships were pointed with fire, and the great red globe of the sun sent crimson light upon the swirling waters of the river and the roofs of the unpicturesque town. Full in this red light, upon the edge of the quay, stood Sydney Capel, and his fellow, Arthur Conyers, guardians of a load of large well-bound kegs and sealed cases in which the colossal treasure lay. In ten minutes the bullion had been stowed in the aft cabin; and when the clerks had shouted "All right!" to those ashore, the tug passed from the docks and steamed quickly up the river—Kess Robinson upon the bridge, a hand named George White at the wheel, the mate, Mike Brennan, fuddled and sleeping in his berth in the fo'castle.

The money had been stowed, as I have written, in the cabin aft; but a few words as to the form of this golden cargo will not come amiss to those who know little of the way in which our great financial houses ship bullion to the Continent. There are many methods. Sometimes the gold takes the shape of ingots, weighing two hundred ounces each; sometimes it is sent in sovereigns, packed in iron-bound cases. A million sovereigns weigh a little more than ten tons. Upon this occasion it had been sent, the larger part in ingots, which were in kegs, the smaller part in sovereigns, which were in the iron-bound chests. Both chests and kegs were stacked in the one cabin of the tug, and it was upon a chest that Sydney Capel, wearing a light travelling coat and cap, sat at the moment the ship passed Gravesend, and began to enter the broader reaches of the river. His fellow-worker, Arthur Conyers—who invariably accompanied him on these occasions—had managed to accommodate himself upon the edge of the captain's bunk, while Messenger, who was talking with expressive animation, leant upon the table beneath the lantern. Looking at the group as a mere spectator, you would have been hard put to imagine it as other than a group of contented idlers, anticipating in the laziness of sea-life a pleasure trip to Flushing. Nor elsewhere on the tug was there the slightest indication of the holocaust so shortly to be offered. The forward look-out chanted his observations with ample briskness; the bullet-headed skipper paced the bridge with a perpetual motion which warranted vigilance; the funnel emitted a dull haze of smoke which would have been a cloud of blackness but for the good Welsh coal. There was not even an episode until the dark fell, and the Chapman light, shining with a great glow for two minutes to leave a void of darkness for one, gave promise of the more open sea at the river's mouth; and of the beginning of that long night of hazard and of death.

As the *Admiral* came opposite to Sheerness, Messenger passed up the companion with a quick look at Capel, and joined the skipper on the bridge.

"Well," he said, "do you make out anything of Kenner's ship?"

"I'm not saying I do," muttered the skipper.

The Prince bit his lip.

"Kenner never was quick," said he. "Light a flare."

A blue light flashed out in the dark, and was answered, but from beyond the Nore.

"He's standing out for the Mouse," said the skipper; "there's no hurt yet."

"'YE'RE BUSY UP THERE, BEDAD'" (p. 55.)

He had more to say, but it remained upon his lips, for when he looked to the deck below, he saw the mate, Mike Brennan, standing there, his eyes winking in the powerful rays of the flare, but a strange curiosity holding him stiff as he glanced from the men upon the bridge to the distant signal, and again from the signal to the men upon the bridge.

The mate was as yet half-sober, but a glimmer of crazy intelligence lighted up his brain · and he stammered out with reckless simplicity—

"Ye're busy up there, bedad!"

This was his remark, and he went to his cabin again with a pretence of stupor and of sullenness which for a moment turned the others from all suspicion of him. For their part, they were too much engrossed in observation of Kenner's yacht, which lay a couple of miles or more ahead of them, to give him much of their thought; and elsewhere upon the tug all was silence, broken only when the look-out hailed the wheel or the bells rang in the engine-room below. The moon had now risen, and was lighting gloriously the white face of the coast of Kent and the dismal marshes of Canvey Island. There was not a cloud in the great silver arc of the heavens; the surface of the river itself was cut by the shadows into rippling, scintillating lakes of light, which showed the black hulls of innumerable barges and the silhouetted shapes of great steamers. And away out towards the coast of France and Belgium the long line of lanterns, revolving, flashing, stationary, marked the path of the deeper Channel, the great water-way to the mighty city which few of those upon the tug were ever to see again.

When they had passed the Nore, leaving the light a cable's length on the starboard bow, it became evident that Kenner was acting with a good deal of discretion. He had run his yacht well past the lightship to wait for the tug, and then had seemed to steer for the North Foreland. This was a mere subterfuge, a precaution which assumed the very unlikely possibility that other ships would observe him and in some measure connect him with the tug. The intention of the manœuvre was not lost either upon Messenger or upon Kess Robinson; and they had scarcely come at the Mouse before the skipper of the tug expressed his satisfaction.

"He's layin' as if for Margate," said he; "and I don't know that he could better it. He'll pick up we in the open fast enough, and the wind's going to hold nor'-west and quiet, or I ain't fit for this job."

"He's certainly standing rather far down Channel," replied Messenger, as he leaned upon the rail and watched the disappearing hull of the American yacht; "but he's got the legs of us at any time, and it's wiser as it is. It wouldn't do to come near him or speak him till we're past Spurn Head, any way; and he's not likely to lose us in a mist this watch, if I'm any judge of weather."

He spoke with some slight quaver of anxiety in his voice, for he was thinking of that curious play of chance which had so ordained it that the Gargantuan emprise of his life was not to be his own work, but that he must rely in some part upon others. Had it been possible that he could have gathered into his own hands the many reins which controlled so ill-assorted a team of rogues and vagabonds, no quake of unpleasant apprehension would have moved him; but he was well aware that the ultimate success of the hazard hung upon the fidelity, the common sense, and the courage of many; and who could answer either for the men in the fo'castle of the tug or for the cut-throats that Kenner had shipped under his flag?

As he minded these things, watching the play of light from the North Foreland and the twinkling lamps in the distant hamlets of Kent, the tug, under the skipper's direction, began slowly to alter her course. She had been laying with her head almost full east; but now she gradually came round, standing for a couple of hours well beyond the remoter shallows of the Maplin Sands, and soon was following a track which brought her far out in the North Sea. The movement was not lost upon the crew, looking to make straight for Flushing, and three of them came from the fo'castle to wait and watch with some expectancy. Even the engineer looked up from his hatchway as though something would mark the departure at the outset, and the whole company maintained a curious silence, lingering for an opening of the drama in which they played such very minor *rôles*.

It was no matter for surprise that the first words of the play were spoken ultimately by one who had been forgotten altogether by this company, in the larger interest which the watching of the other yacht promoted. Mike Brennan had gone down to his cabin again after the moment of the flare; but now, of a sudden, when all aboard were gazing over the starboard bow at the evolutions of the *Semiramis*, the mate appeared at the foot of the bridge, armed with a great bludgeon of iron; and behind him there stood Arthur Conyers, the elderly clerk, who had drawn his revolver and wore the aspect of a man puckered up for great emergencies. And it was the voice of the mate, then raised in a clear and unmistakably meaning tone, which awakened the others to the situation.

"Skipper," said the man, with one foot upon the ladder and a hand upon the rail, "I've a question to ask av ye concerning the course. Will ye hear it now or will I be waiting?"

At the first sound of the mate's voice the skipper glanced down to the scene below. Temper and fear alike held him as the moment of the spectacle dawned upon him. Yet he spoke with some command, even before Messenger—who had reckoned up the danger at a look—could give counsel or take action.

"Mike Brennan," said he, "it's not the first time ye're concerning yourself with my affairs. Put yer dirty body in bed before I kick it there!"

The contempt of this was hard enough, but

mightily rash, for it sent hot blood coursing through the Irishman's veins, and the skipper's lips were scarce shut before the mate had sprung up the ladder, and with one blow from the bar had sent him hurtling over the paddle-box into the sea, where he sank as a bag of rock, and left almost unruffled the long wave that engulfed him.

From that moment—as the scant record bears witness—the deck of the tug became a shambles. The greed of blood consumed the Irishman until he raved uncontrollably, and, making a mighty cut at Messenger, he missed his aim, and fell headlong to the deck below, where now the crack of Conyers' revolver was heard. The man, with his eyes open to the trap he had fallen into, had lost all self-restraint, and fired hap-hazard, the bullets singing above the heads of the tug's crew, who lay huddled together by the fore-hatch, or skimming the deck, or burying themselves in the bulwarks, or ringing upon the cowls. And through it all he did not cease to cry out with all his voice, so that the tug rang with his shouts, and, believing that Capel was with him in the work, he appealed to him, and to Messenger upon the bridge.

"Capel," he cried, "for God's sake, shoot, man! There's murder done here—murder, I tell you! They're killing the mate! Do you hear me? We're in a trap, I tell you! in a trap, by Heaven!"

But Capel made no answer—he was cowering and sobbing aft; and when the honest fellow had cried himself hoarse and emptied the chambers of his revolver, a new sound of firing burst up by the forecastle, where two of the crew were using their pistols at the mate, but to small purpose. Brennan, staggering with the dizziness of his fall, had got what shelter he could under the shadow of the paddle-box; but presently he ran with his bar at the three forward, and the skull of one cracked like a globe, while the other two fell howling down the hatchway. In that moment this man and Conyers were master of the deck, and only Messenger, who had watched the whole scene from the bridge, was powerful to raise a hand.

Unto this point there had been little danger from Conyers, who, in his wild blundering and hap-hazard suspicion, had left Messenger alone, scarce understanding whether he were friend or foe. But when he had emptied his revolver and stood fumbling to refill the chambers in the black patch of shadow which the wheel cast, Messenger sprang down lightly from the bridge, and appeared before him as a swift apparition from the dark.

"Come," said he, in that peculiarly stern voice he could command on occasion, "I think you've done enough for one night. Put down that pistol."

Conyers obeyed him, as the weak ever obey the strong, even in the moment of danger.

"Now," continued the other in the same tone, "march aft, and don't come up again until I call you, unless you want a body full of holes."

The man, weary of the butchery, and suffering the terrors of reaction, went to the companion without a word and descended it, when the other locked the cabin-door upon him and turned round to see Capel's pallid face and trembling form.

"Capel," said he, "I'm thinking you're a big man in a difficulty. How came it that this devil got loose?"

"It was the mate," whimpered the other, "the mate, upon my word; he came down to the cabin when you had gone and swore he'd shoot me if I moved. Then he told Conyers—you know what—and they went forward together."

"Just as I thought. Well, someone's got to make it level with that mate, and there's no time to be drivelled away either; I'm going forward, and you're coming with me."

Capel had little relish for the job, but he was nigh as much afraid to stay as to advance; and he hid himself in Messenger's shadow and skulked forward with the new master of the ship. The mate, now scared and giddy, had thrown down his bar, and was sitting upon a ballast chest; but he looked up at the soft sound of the footsteps, and sprang to his feet with a ferocious cry.

"Houly saints," said he, grasping his weapon, "it's yerself, ye mouldy scounthrel, that I've been waitin' to be at—may the Lord give me strength!"

He stood now full upright, the fine picture of a man in the moonlight; and at the sound of his voice the crew in the fo'castle showed for a moment at the hatch again. Had Messenger been alone with him, he would have ended the business then and there with his revolver, but he feared the crew, to whom the mate was even then something of a hero; and he knew that the sound of repeated firing might bring ships upon the tug. In this, however, was his mistake; and even as he stood, with the irresolution of an instant, the Irishman whirled the great bar round and made a mighty stroke at his head. But the blow had been dealt with too great a vigour; the smooth iron slipped from the man's grasp; the bar hurtled through the air with terrible force. It passed above the shoulder of Messenger, who had dropped upon one knee, and, missing him, struck Sydney Capel so full across the face that the bones of his forehead cracked at the blow—and he fell, with the life out of him, prone upon the deck. For a moment the horrid tragedy held the others speechless; the mate shivered as though intense cold had gripped him; the crew crouched backward as from a madman. Messenger alone kept his wits; and, before the now unarmed Irishman had got his courage again, he hit him with his fist and felled him, striking him again and again with heavy blows, until the man had no more sense in him than a log of wood. Then he called for a length of rope, and binding him hand and foot, left him as he lay and went back to the bridge.

The moment was one of the most critical in this strange man's history. The most trivial curiosity of a drunken sailor had in one half-hour threatened the giant superstructure of design he had created with so much labour. Here he was almost full in the track of ships plying to the Scheldt and to Holland, by no means ready for the transfer of the bullion to the yacht, lacking the animal cleverness of the dead Kess Robinson, with the deck of the tug bloodstained and his partner in the felony no longer living either to participate in success or to share the shame of failure. Indeed, his predicament was one of vast dangers, for the crew of the *Admiral* had become paralysed with the precipitancy of the fight, and crouched in their hammocks daft with terror; the engineer went to his work mechanically; the man White, who had come back to the wheel, muttered and crooned like a hag at a distaff. Not one of them had the veriest suggestion of action or anything but stupefying fear in him; not one but shuddered every time he turned his eyes towards the spot where the dead man lay. Messenger, even with his wire-knit nerves, suffered for some time the contagion of the terror. He found himself pacing the bridge with nervous strides, or pausing in keen thought, or gazing out seawards, where the sweep of the horizon gave him sparse encouragement. Kenner's yacht still lay a couple of miles away from them; but there was a fleet of North Sea smacks upon the port quarter, and a couple of steamers stood out clear some three miles away in their course. Under other circumstances that was not the time to have acted; the danger of remark and observation was too palpable: the sinking of the tug might even be reported in London before the morning watch; yet the man had a haunting wish to quit the scene of the deadly brawl at the first moment possible; he gained a new terror from the want of talk, and at last he called the engineer, a Scotchman, by name Alec Johnson, and set upon his questioning.

"Well," said he, "this is pretty work for a beginning."

"Aye, it's a sorra spectacle, man, and yer no cutting a fine appearance, may I tell ye," replied Johnson, as he stood at the foot of the ladder and hesitated to mount it.

"I don't want your opinions," said Messenger testily, "but your notions, if you've got any. Do you think it's time to be moving from this ship?"

The engineer shrugged his shoulders, suggesting his indifference.

"Well," said he, "you're dawdlin' in queersome company. I've no stomach myself to jawk wi' the dead, but the sea's muckle full of ships for what ye were thinking of."

"That's true. You've some glimmer of intelligence, any way," answered Messenger, as he resumed his sentry-like perambulation, pausing only at the second turn to continue his argument.

"Is all right below when the time comes?" he asked with some anxiety. "We've got to see this hulk out of sight five minutes after we leave her, any way."

"Man, ye can rest on that," said the Scotchman; "she'll just flichter and go down like a bag wi' a stone in her; and look ye, there'll be mist afore the morn, and it may give ye shelter."

"So there will," cried the other, as he turned away, leaving the engineer to go below. And for a couple of hours the tug steamed onward, the thud of her paddles the only sound, her decks untenanted save for the solemn, wakeful man upon the bridge, and the moody, inert, sullen fellow who took the wheel. Day had now broken, with cold grey light and piercing white mist which settled humidly upon ship and watchers, and hid the near sea so that neither the yacht of the American, nor such packets or smacks as lay by them, could be seen. But anon a great wave of dull red light split the vapour through, floating it on wings of radiant colour, or dissolving it so that at last the waste of green water all capped with playing flecks of foam, lay clear to the view; and the invigorating freshness of morning seemed to give a new call to the labours of the day. That hour, so superb in its breath of strength, so life-giving to him who rises from long sleep, was an hour of new fear to those that remained in the shambles of the tug. As the sun rose, it seemed to lighten the face of the dead man, who lay as he had fallen, with a hideous, ghastly glare upon him, so that the crew, coming with a new courage a little way aft, shrunk back and implored to be set free; or cried out that they would all be taken, yet feared

E

to touch the dread thing and send it to the sea, which engulfs the dead in so sure a resting-place. Messenger himself understood, with his usual perception, that the tension could not be long endured, and at the change of the watch (there being but one steamer other than the yacht in their wake, and she many miles on their port bow), he suddenly gave the order to go about, and stood boldly for the *Semiramis*, though all the risk of the action was apparent to him.

The men, raving with delight at the thought of release from the unendurable prison, now came scampering up their ladder, though they did not venture abaft the fore deck; and in a moment all was activity. There were but five of the crew remaining, and of these one was almost a boy, who was called "Billy," and reckoned half-dolt, half-idiot. As for the mate, who had lain near the forehatch apparently insensible, and bound since the fray, he was forgotten by all in the thirst for change at whatever risk or price. The new course was, it may be imagined, at once observed by those on the *Semiramis*, who fell to signalling; and in a run of ten minutes the tug had come alongside the big yacht, and being grappled, twenty hands hoisted the bullion to the crane, and guided it over the aft hatchway. It was no time for greeting, no time for anything but a babel of voices, a quick pumping of donkey engines, a bustle, a confusion, and a riot when the men from the tug tumbled pell-mell upon the yacht, and the dead were forgotten, and the bound man below had no mercy from the hungry wolves who clustered about the gold.

The exciting work occupied some twenty minutes in performance, and having been accomplished, Roger Burke, upon the bridge of the *Semiramis*, roared the order—"Let her go!" The tug swung away from the hull of the greater vessel almost with his words, and a few powerful strokes from the twin screws separated the doomed ship and the other by several cables' lengths. At the distance they waited for the end; but before the end could be there was an apparition upon the bridge of the *Admiral* which sent pallor to the faces of the exultant crew, and drew from the men cries of rage and of apprehension. For suddenly, as the tug drifted, the man who had been bound and forgotten, Mike Brennan, the mate, appeared by the wheel, and with frenzied imprecations called threats from Heaven upon the watchers and their ship. During one moment he stood, and then there came a great dull roar as of a mighty explosion in the engine-room below him; and the little steamer, heeling to the shock, cocked her stern above the playing waves, and in the next instant had plunged below them.

With the gurgle of the hull the mate disappeared; but as he went the voice of Billy, the daft boy, was heard in triumphant exclamation—

"I cut him free. I did it. Who'll hear Billy? Oh, dam clever, dam clever!"

The tug sank with his words, and while many of the crew called upon the skipper to search the waters for the spectre of the bridge, others observed that the strange steamer, which had been an hour ago but a speck on the horizon, loomed large on their starboard quarter, and Burke would wait for no man.

"Mate or no mate," said he, "I'm getting, and I guess ez there'll be a tight run as it is. If that ship's took the bearings of this business, there'll be half the cruisers floating on our track afore night, and that ain't my particular fancy, not much."

And at his command the *Semiramis* bounded forward to her doom.

CHAPTER V.

THE THIRD DAY AFTER.

IT was upon the evening of the third day after the going down of the tug, at two bells in the watch, that the *Semiramis* entered the Minch, and began her passage southward. She had run at a high speed, but under no forced draught, and with all possible economy of fuel, up the North Sea to Duncansby Head. Thence rounding Cape Wrath (but at a great distance from the light to escape all observation) she had struck boldly past the Western Isles on her ultimate purpose of making the open Atlantic. And she was then ploughing her way upon a stiff swell, and against a full south wind, to the less dangerous waterway of the greater ocean.

During three days all the fever and unrest of inexplicable fear had sat heavy upon her crew; and in some part upon those most concerned in her fortunes. It had been a voyage girt about with apprehension, pursued in foreboding, matured in ignorance. Unmindful of the bulky cases of gold which lumbered the great saloon, and in which masters and men were at no distant date to participate, the hands had not ceased to ask themselves, What do those in London know ? How far are we wise to hug shores like this ? When will the pursuit begin ? To their blunt intelligence it seemed the apex of folly that the *Semiramis* should, even for the space of a day, haunt the confined waters of the Scottish coast. Urged on by Johnson, the engineer of the sunken tug, and quietly encouraged by the evident restlessness of Kenner, they stated their views on the quarter-deck, or sulked in their own fo'castle, or even contemplated such an outbreak as would have ended the business upon the spot.

It was not difficult to realise that the cargo of money was to such as these an all-potent temptation. Although the precise means by which it had come into the power of Messenger and Kenner were unknown to them, its presence in the saloon was like a loadstone that drew them abaft the funnel irresistibly, and allowed them to think and speak of naught else but bullion. So strong was the temptation that on the second day the hand, George White, who had been one of Robinson's men, was found in the cabin rolling over a keg of ingots in his effort to open it, and, being taken in the act by Burke, was ordered out for immediate punishment.

"I'll make an example of ye ez'll go right round the ship," said the skipper, as the man stood before him; "an' if that don't cure, I'll empty my shot-gun in yer hide."

"Ye can't touch me," said the man sullenly; "I ain't signed for you, and I don't see no one here as is going to make me."

The hands had crowded round the engine-room hatch (where the discussion was held) at the sound of loud voices; and some of them murmured at the man's plea and agreed with him.

"Ye can't touch him," said they; "he's none o' yourn, and we're all his way."

Burke looked at them very quietly as they spoke, and, one of the fellows approaching him in a threatening attitude, he suddenly whipped out a great army revolver from his hip-pocket and hit the fellow such a crash over the head with it that he went reeling backwards until his heel caught in the iron of a glass-light, and he fell his whole length upon the deck.

"Now," said the skipper, "I guess ez I'm open to any more arguments o' that sort. Is there them among ye, belike, as will step forward an' state 'em!"

They all slunk away at the words, the man White seeking to shuffle off with the others; but Burke suddenly held him with a great grip and shook him so that his teeth chattered. "A-goin' for'ard to sleep it off awhile, was ye?" said he; "then I'm darned if I don't wake ye up a bit! Here! lash him up to the rail some of ye. It ain't no Queen's ship, ain't it? You didn't sign no papers for me, didn't ye? Wal, by Jerusalem, I'm a-going to sign 'em for ye and seal 'em, too!"

Four lascars, who had watched the whole scene with an Oriental indifference, at once stepped out to obey Burke's orders. Messenger and Kenner had kept back during the brawl; holding themselves altogether apart from the crew throughout the voyage; but Fisher witnessed the scene with indignation bubbling upon his lips. And while he watched, having the sense to keep his tongue still, the burly seaman was triced up by his arms to the boards of the bridge; his feet were lashed to the ring of a ballast-chest; his coat was torn off his back; and thus hanging by his arms, and almost bearing the whole of his weight, he received his punishment. Fifty swinging lashes from a whip with three leathern thongs descended upon his bare back, the sound of the blows echoing through the ship with the sound of a cane that beats heavily upon a board; and at each blow the man roared like a bull, while his cries for mercy were as pitiful as the wails of a child in pain. When they took him down he had fainted; but Burke kicked his body with his foot, and, squirting a mouthful of his filthy tobacco upon the deck, he said—

"So ye didn't sign, my son! Well, that's my mark instead, en I reckon ez it'll take ye a week or two to wipe it off. Throw him into a bunk one of yer, and if he ez got any more views when he wakes, I calculate I'm ready to hear 'em on the same terms."

The scene was concluded in a wistful hush—the hush of men obeying, but not obedient. Burke's ferocity had cowed all spectators; for the moment it had overridden the danger, and it had sent Hal Fisher to the saloon with the gloomiest face possible. During the three days gone, the lad had seemed to live in a hazy dream, a dream which had brought to him many pictures and many episodes—but chiefly shadows of impressions, as dreams will. He remembered that he had slept in his bunk two nights before to be awakened in the morning watch by a great commotion and business upon the deck; but when he tried his door he found it locked; and it was only after some hours, and when he had slept again, that he reached the deck to learn that they were standing right out in the North Sea, and that many strange events had happened in the betweentime. For one thing his friend Messenger greeted him directly he had mounted the companion, and while he stood gaping at the sight of new faces and wondering at the amazing fact of their appearance, the Prince had slapped him upon the back, and begun his explanation.

"Hal," said he, "you didn't look to see me this morning."

"I didn't look for any such luck," replied Hal, giving him grip for grip.

"Well, what did I tell you three days ago? The fact is, I've been driven almost wild with work since three months ago—and now it's over, or nearly over."

"And I suppose you'll condescend to tell me

something?" suggested Fisher, with his old doubts upon him.

"Why, of course, I'm going to tell you everything—and that's told in half-a-dozen words. In the first place, we're going somewhere, and it's no twenty-four hours' pleasure trip—that you can see; in the second, we've got something on board that we wouldn't sell for a shilling a pound, Hal; it's a freight of money!"

He almost whispered the last words; and, as he saw the boy's surprise, he laughed cheerily, and linking his arm with the youngster's, he began to pace the deck abaft the engine-room.

"Yes," said he, picking up the thread without more ado, "Kenner and I are in for a big thing, old man. We're trying to run this freight to Buenos Ayres in the interest of people I must not name. It's a big job; and the men for'ard can't exactly be trusted as though they'd come from a seminary. We may have to fight; in any case, we've got to use our sea-legs. And you'll have to stand by us, as I said four days ago; but I needn't ask you if you'll do that?"

Fisher listened to the clumsy lie as a schoolboy listens to a tar's yarn. The truth was that Messenger almost made the tale as he went; for he had to satisfy the boy's curiosity somehow, and certainly he met with no embarrassing questions. His pupil had seen little of life, and the obvious absurdity of the notion that there was unusual danger in carrying money to the Argentine never dawned upon his untrained mind.

He only thought that here he was plunged in a moment into as good an adventure as ever he heard, and he answered with fine enthusiasm—

"Stand by you! Why, of course. Is there anyone else I should stand by if it isn't you?'

The mutual confidence would have been beautiful if it had not been all on one side—an exchange of frankness for lies, of love for a selfish liking. Yet Messenger had the greatest satisfaction at that moment in having at least one honest hand with him on the ship; and, if the truth be told, he trusted the boy alone of all the company. Kenner was a tricky rogue, who would turn upon him at any moment; Burke was a ranting bully who—then, at any rate—had the command of the situation; it lay upon the Englishman to trust to his wits and fine talent to come out of the undertaking even with his life. In such a situation the boy he had before befriended could befriend him; and befriend him he did, as the development of the narrative proves all conclusively.

The confidence between man and boy being established, and the incident of the flogging being forgotten, the first three days of the flight of the *Semiramis* lacked any episode of moment. There was unrest upon the yacht, mutterings, occasional outbursts of temper; but, beyond these, no *tour de force* on the part of the men; no event of any interest upon the sea. So far, indeed, did the yacht stand off the shore that the light of Cape Wrath was not even seen; and, Burke believing that the notion of pursuit was an old woman's dream, they passed through the Minch on the evening of the third day, and at eight bells in the forenoon watch they sighted Skerryvore Lighthouse many miles distant on their port quarter. From that point they shaped a course west by south to run past Malin Head; and although they passed some steamers of considerable size which were making for Scottish ports, they stood as far from them as possible, and spoke none; nor, indeed, invited any observation.

This was the situation on the third day, and it did not alter until midnight, when Fisher came on deck to take the middle watch. It had been agreed by the cabin party that they should, one by one, take duty at the head of the companion, lest the great temptation of the gold should lure any of the crew aft; and this duty the boy shared loyally with the others. For the matter of that not one of them aboard took his clothes off from the first hour of the flight, nor did any of them let his revolver go far from his sight and grip. As for Fisher, he had been given a couple of pistols, and told to shoot down any man who attempted to enter the saloon without an open account of himself; and while he might have hesitated literally to obey this order, Messenger and Kenner got nearer to sleep during his watch than at any other time.

The boy being thus upon guard, and quiet reigning in the ship, the fourth day began with squalls from the north-west and a tumbling sea which spread sheets of bubbling foam upon the fore-deck and sent gushing streams from the lee scuppers. The night was very dark, with mountains of heavy cloud which hid the heavens, and for the first two hours of the watch there was no moon. It was even bitterly cold, as with the cold of later winter; and Fisher, who paced the quarter-deck with many lively thoughts, shivered in his oilskins, and suppressed his yawns with difficulty. Burke was at that time sleeping, and his subordinate—a thin and very humble man, named Parker—paced the bridge; but aft, the whistling of the sharp gusts in the shrouds alone broke the stillness.

Once or twice, as the lad strode up and down in the darkness, he had thoughts that others moved upon the deck near him; but his nerves were overwrought and weary, and the singing of a rope, or the thud of the heavier seas, set them troubling. As the bells were struck until four were numbered, the depth of night was more intensified; the wind was shriller; the motion of the yacht more irregular. He found himself hanging to the rail at the top of the hatchway for sheer footing, and was there haunted by innumerable phantoms of suspicion to which the bleakness of the night gave birth. There were moments when he was certain that he heard, at the fall of the gale, whispers from the darker places by the bulwarks; other moments when he conjured up visions of figures, dark and armed, lurking behind the skylight. Or again, he suffered from that illogical conviction, which many suffer in solitude, that someone stood by him in the dark and was about to speak to him; and this feeling was so strong that he was almost of a mind to awaken Messenger and the others, but did not, fearing to look a coward.

In this approach to panic he watched yet a spell, when of a sudden, chancing to look down the higher line of the deck, he was absolutely sure that all was not a dream. There, almost at his feet, the hunched-up figure of a man lay timidly, the figure of a man waiting to speak, but lacking words. He looked at the man for a moment, whipping out his revolver as he did so, but when he had his hand upon the trigger, the watcher rose and gripped his arm.

"Billy no hurt," he chattered; "you don't shoot Billy! They cut your throat jess now, cut everyone. Billy know, he see 'em; oh, he see 'em!"

In this mood the daft lad raved whisperingly; but the other stood wondering and still with the sudden alarm. Should he descend the companion silently, or should he fire a shot and bring the sleepers to their feet? For a moment he did not know, and, as he waited, twenty figures—the more part armed with knives and iron bars, but three carrying revolvers—came with cat-like tread from the deck-house amidships to the poop.

CHAPTER VI.

LIGHT—BUT NOT OF DAWN.

THE purpose of the men being no longer hid, Fisher set himself quickly to action. He fired three rounds from his Colt, and then bawled with all his strength for those below to come up. The sing of the bullets held back the throng while one could count ten, but no longer. They had not further need of stealth, and began to shout savagely, hugging close, the one to the other, for encouragement. Their answer to the pistol-shots was a discharge of their own weapons and many imprecations. Had they come on yet another ten paces they had all been atop of the ladder and swarming down to the cabin; but of a sudden they held together with a great cry, and many of them fell upon their knees in an extremity of terror which no phrase could convey. And upon them there shone a great light, full of whiteness and dazzling—a light which came in focussed radiance across the sea, and cut a path of spreading brightness out of the very blackness of the fullest night.

The light fell upon them, as I say, and for many minutes they could neither speak, nor move, nor did any man ask his neighbour, whence comes the terror? It lay on many of their minds that some visitation of God had opened the sky to shed light upon their work; and until reason had rolled back upon her balance, they had neither tongues nor ears. But anon, when Burke and Messenger had come running up from the aft cabin, and the skipper had observed the dark hull of a cruiser, whose search-light played upon the yacht from a point some two miles away on the starboard quarter, they passed from their fear to wild oaths; and as the sound of a gun rolled over the sea, the white faces and bright eyes of the whole of them turned quickly to that place where the danger was to be observed.

So far as can be learned from a later narrative, the first man to speak in that moment of panic was Burke, the skipper. Suddenly, as with the sound of a wild animal roaring, his orders echoed through the ship.

"Curse you for a parcel of lazy swine, get up!" he roared. "Get up, I say! Do you think ez it's the Day of Judgment, ye Chicago hogs? All hands on deck and to their places, ye white-livered lubbers! Move, or, by thunder, I'll come down and move ye!"

They awoke at this, moving to their places. A double watch tumbled into the stoke-hole; a couple of gunners cleared the three-inch Nordenfelt guns, which were at the bow and amidships. In five minutes the thought of the contemplated scuffle for

"UPON THEM THERE SHONE A GREAT LIGHT" (*p.* 79).

the gold was forgotten. Bells were ringing, orders were bawled. The forced draught began to roar in the furnaces. The whole deck, which had been a hive of silence ten minutes before, now echoed with movement, with voices, with the clamour of action. Nor was there need ot explanation; instinctively all aboard knew that the pursuit was no longer a possibility, but an actuality; that by some plain chain of circumstances those upon land had heard of their filibustering, and were seeking them. Men passed each other in those moments with scarce opportunity to exchange an opinion; but those that spoke uttered such convictions as, "She's after us, for sure!" or such questions as, "Be they going to take us?"—and a gloom settled sternly upon the more part of them. But they worked with an unquestionable will, though their new fidelity was as much a matter of self-preservation as their erstwhile treachery had been the outcome of covetousness.

While there was this hubbub of disorder upon the decks below, there was upon the bridge a display of fine command and skilled seamanship. Burke, who ruled with resonant voice, and was easy to be heard above the wind, had eyes both for his own men and the plunging cruiser; Messenger gripped the rail and smoked a cigar with easy assurance; Kenner was restless, and dared a pessimistic forecast at unseemly intervals.

"Wal," said he, "I said it was a swinging job at

F

Monaco three months ago, and it looks like setting me up in the prophet line."

Messenger listened to him with a childlike smile playing about his mouth, and answered—

"Why not go to bed till we're out of it? They tell me that some men get wonderfully good notions with their heads under the clothes."

"Maybe," replied the American, "and maybe 1 squirm. But don't you see he's drivin' us right agen the Irish coast; and where are ye then?"

"Why, right along the Irish coast, I suppose, as you say so."

Kenner stood before him and looked him up and down.

"Prince," said he, "I guess if I rubbed ice agen you you wouldn't melt it. Hang me if your mother didn't feed you on snowballs."

"Perhaps," said Messenger; "anyway, she taught me that you don't go far on a harum-scarum, and it's true."

"But," argued the other, getting angry, "don't you see, man, that once she's forced us shoreward there'll be twenty ships on our track. You don't seem to take it in."

"That's likely," replied Messenger, as he struck a fusee. "There are few things, however, I don't take in when the opportunity comes. The fact is, I wasn't born a skipper, and I'm too old to turn to the job. Don't you think it's as well to leave the business to Burke?

This latter word expressed the whole of the man. Since he had got the money upon the ship, he knew that the better part of his work was done. He was not a seaman; it rested with Burke, the skipper, to get the bullion into port. He could only wait and watch, and take from chance the gift apportioned to him. Kenner, on the other hand, was a man who concerned himself in every person's business, and did nobody's. He envied the Prince his *sang-froid*, his illimitable calm, his assurance; and when he could get nothing out of him he went to the skipper, who had his hand upon the communicator, and renewed his absurdities.

The situation was at that time very critical. Dark still held down upon the sea, save in that arc of whiteness which the search-light cast. The wind blew almost a full gale; green seas swept the foredecks and threatened to flood the fo'castle. The yacht trembled from stem to stern as every foam-capped mount of water struck her and went swinging away down her whole length. So great was her speed that she scarce rode a sea, but ploughed through it with foam-spurts shooting up incessantly above her prow and a quivering of her plates which sent fear palpitating in all who felt it. There was no thought then, however, either of tempests or of the great rolling volumes of foam and water which were driven by the wind in mighty devouring masses until they struck the iron coast of Donegal, fifty miles away. All eyes were turned upon the cruiser there, pursuing as a hideous phantom of the night; clinging to them, despite the vast use of fuel; seeming to have gained upon them every time there was a lift of the night or any show of her beaming light. And when another hour passed, the conviction, which had been growing since the beginning of it, became emphasised, and men expressed it, crying, "We're took! Heaven help us, we're took!" and clinging together as those upon whom a vengeance comes to find them unready.

And thus the night passed, and the angry dawn rose above the wildness of the sea.

CHAPTER VII.

"A TEMPEST DROPPING FIRE."

Day broke slowly, with a low mount of black cloud upon the horizon and but scant abatement of the wind, which began to blow again from the fuller west. Torrents of cooling rain now poured upon the decks of the *Semiramis*, and were sport for the hurricane, which tossed them hither and thither in blinding sheets. All over the angry waste of water, the loud contest of the thundering rollers was to be heard and seen; booming out with the dull roar of rushing cataracts; or spurting high in silvery cascades where the greater waves were checked. The darkness of night was scarcely worse than the gloom of the new dawn—a gloom of lowering black vapour and raging sea, of the mournful wailing of the wind and suggested desolation.

When the light, such as it was, gave clearer outline to the worn face of the Atlantic, those upon the bridge of the yacht looked down upon a strange scene. There were but two ships on the sea with them; and of these one was the cruiser, which plunged through the swelling tempest a couple of miles away on their starboard quarter; the other was a full-rigged ship, now running under a storm-jib and reefed topsails towards the Irish coast. For the rest, there was but the restless flash of white water, the swirl of giant billows, the crash of breaking rollers, the hemisphere of gathering cloud.

With such an environment, the customary spirit of Burke's crew was altogether lacking. For the most part the men lay huddled together just abaft the fore-hatch, and had eyes for nothing but the cruiser, which seemed to hold the yacht so easily, yet could gain nothing upon her. They had even ceased to ask the question, "Shall we be took?" but remained inert and hopeless as the chase was pursued and the situation remained unchanged. Nor did those upon the bridge speak, but took it as men at war with chance, but to whom chance is no task-master. This tension was almost insupportable for some hours while the yacht plunged onward at a terrible pace, and thrilled and quivered as a woman who has received a blow. It might have endured to the end but for the cook, one-legged Joe, to whom all things were but meat for the pot, who came up from the galley and began, after his usual habit, to stump the deck, and call the hands to breakfast, as a muezzin calls to prayer in the cities of the Prophet. Joe was a half-caste; and his jerky step upon the fo'castle was the surest signal to merriment forward under placid circumstances; but on that morning of the fourth day it was little welcome, and for some time, at any rate, it met with curt response.

"Be gor!" cried the man, as he hopped up and down his fine balance disregarding the vigour of the lurches, "be gor! if this don't beat cold rum. A sight of gemmelen what hab forgotten eight bells; and all for a bit of a ship that Joe wouldn't go for to jump over, sahs—not for to jump over!"

He stopped his antics before the Scotchman, Johnson, who was holding fast to the shrouds of the short foremast and surveying him with withering contempt.

"Man," said he to the cook, "ye're ower blithesome for the time of day, I'm thinking. Have ye no stomach for yon?"

"Sah," replied Joe, "you warm the innar man, sah; you gib 'em plenty stomach by-and-by; you gib 'em what young gemmelen call hot-pot and slops, sah—Joe know; he smell war, sah, while him a long way off."

With this he fell to hopping up and down again on the ill-made steel-leg, which served him at once as a means of ambulation, and, as the crew declared, in place of a cooking-spoon when the need was. For the matter of that, he bawled so lustily and with such effect that a few men presently turned down to breakfast, and Burke followed their example, leading Kenner and the others with him.

It was not the hour when men might think of food—but the skipper knew that long and arduous labour was before them all; and, for himself, he showed as good an appetite as a roysterer at a village fair, and washed down great hunks of meat with frequent potations from a bottle of Hollands.

"That's the stuff ez'll warm you best for a picnic such ez this is," said he, as he pushed the bottle to the others. "None o' your slops and fizzing pison fer me, Prince, nor yet coffee neither; I guess Rome wasn't took on that sort, en we ain't a-going to git this yere yallow cargo ashore on it no more'n they could—give me spirit."

"You appear to be helping yourself," said Messenger, upon whom the excitement of the moment had no power for impression; "I don't see where we come in, anyway. I shall take coffee, if there's any to be got."

"Wal," interposed Kenner, "so should I if it wasn't an occasion. But if this don't beat a birthday fête, I never knew one. Blarm me! but I can think on liquor."

He consoled himself with the conclusion, and fell to work, holding a glass in one hand and food in the other, since the yacht rolled so terribly that the swinging lamp above the table threatened to strike the skylight at every lurch. In reality his craving for strong drink was the outcome of the raging anxiety—nay, even fear—which consumed him, and, indeed, all of them but the Prince, who made as good a breakfast as a hunting squire, and did not cease a gentle irony and banter through the whole of the meal.

"Burke," said he in one of the intervals, "I want to know what you're going to do if we can't show that ship yonder a clean pair of heels before night?"

"What em I going to do?" asked Burke. "Wal, that's a fair question, and I'll give you a fair reply—I dun know!"

"Perhaps you can tell us, Kenner?" said Messenger, turning to the American. "You think on liquor, you know."

"That's so," replied Kenner; "but I ain't full up yet. I guess I can tell you one thing, though, my boy: if this hulk don't show a couple of knots more in the next two hours it's nothing stronger than skilly that most of us will lap, and that only for a spell."

Fisher, who listened to the conversation eagerly, looked up at the words and asked—

"What does he mean, Prince?"

"Means ez he'll have to dance the polker with no parket floorin' under him," replied Burke, who took up the conversation.

"And he means also," said Messenger quietly, "that this skipper of ours is a sillier man than his bulk gives you any idea of."

"What's that?" cried Burke, bringing his huge fist upon the table with Gargantuan strength. "You're going to take that back, I reckon, en quick."

Messenger leant against the cushions of his seat one of his hands resting upon a case of ingots, and he replied to the man with the suggestion of a leer. But Burke was fuddled with the liquor, and he half rose from the table and asked with a hiccough—

"Who commands aboard this ship?"

"Sober men," replied Messenger quietly.

"I'm asking you for a plain word en no roundabout. Do I command ye, or do I not?"

"You may command who the devil you like," answered Messenger testily; "but if you say two words to me, I'll pitch you off your own bridge."

The threat was mildly said, but the slim man who spoke looked so well able to answer for his words that the great skipper sank back upon his seat with a senseless smile and turned the conversation.

"Well!" said he. "I always knew ye for a ornery one, and if anyone says as there's harm in ye I give him the lie, the straight lie. The question is, What do yer want? I've done all ez I ken do, I reckon. Ken you do more?—will you tell me that?"

But no one answered him, and the Prince began to speak to Kenner.

"Kenner," said he, "every cock on his own dunghill, and every skipper on his own bridge so long as he's got the wits of a mule. The situation is as clear to me as that coffee-pot there. The ship over there is trying to drive us to the mouth of the Channel. If she has the luck, the 'In memoriam' notices will be up for all of us inside a month. Personally, I've no love for assisting at funerals, and I've less hankering to be the chief business in one. Yet it's quite clear to me that, since they've got the legs of us, we must either find the open ocean, or leave the thing now, like a lot of old women trooping out of an excursion train. You told me that you could show heels to anything swimming; but you can't, and that's the weak spot in the whole of it——"

"Stay a bit," cried Kenner, "you're not at a political garden party, and I don't foller. I said this yacht could do twenty-two knots in a free sea; and so she can—I'll go my last dime on it."

"That may be," replied Messenger; "but, whatever she can do, the other is up to it. You've got eyes, and you can see as well as I can."

Burke looked up suddenly at the words, and chimed in—

"She's doin' twenty-two knots now, if that'll help you."

"Possibly," replied Messenger; "but I'm not interested. What I want to learn is the exact time and place for the shoot into the open?"

"Wal, if it's shooting you're after, you'll get plenty of that directly you put across her bows," said Kenner expressively; and the skipper gave a great guffaw at his words, as a drunken man will ever laugh at a hand's breadth of pleasantry.

The laugh was still upon his lips when the roar of a gun echoed over the sea, and the three men sprang to their feet together.

"They've begun it already!" said Burke; and in a moment he shook off the grip of the drink, and bounded up the companion. Thither the others followed him, to see a cloud of smoke enveloping the pursuing cruiser, and their own men lying about the deck in a depth of fear and craven sullenness which surpassed anything they had yet been guilty of.

CHAPTER VIII.

SOUTH FOR CORUNNA.

THE hour which the men had spent in the cabin witnessed but little change in the path of the hurricane. There was, perhaps, a slight abatement in the velocity of the wind, and the black banks of cloud had burst asunder into great masses of rolling humidity, which showed other masses, and these of a purer grey or white, in the distance beyond them. Yet there was scarce a glimmer of sun, save for a space of five or six minutes, when a fan of spectral light shot down upon the green of the sea, dazzling with hues of sparkling brightness; but promising no fall of the gale nor moderation of the raging tempest. Everywhere the whited wave-caps tumbled joyously upon one another; everywhere the gigantic rollers made hills and valleys of green water, which swept the yacht and her pursuer onward, as they would have swept a faggot of sticks or a board of wood. It was a scene worthy of the mighty grandeur of the Atlantic, of all the traditions of tempests which sweep upon her; but it had little charm for those upon the *Semiramis*, nor, as one may know, for the hands of the cruiser, which then bore the whole brunt of the seas in the work which had fallen to her.

Burke's first question, when he got upon the bridge, was one concerning the gun which had just been fired, and whose smoke still lay upon the sea.

"You there!" he cried. "Was that shell or was it blarney?"

"It was a shell, sir," said the mate Parker; "it just cleared the lifeboat davits, sir, may it please you."

"By thunder, it don't please me!" cried Burke. "What are they doing down below, the scum?"

At the words, he shouted down the tube for more coal, though the men were already reeling under the work, and the furnaces were white hot with an irradiant heat, which was almost unbearable in the stokehole. To hope for greater speed was the dream of a dreamer; yet, despite all that was being done, the two vessels maintained their relative places, and it had already become clear that, if there was no coming-between of chance, the yacht must be taken.

When Burke had exhausted his breath in childish abuse to his engineers, the humble mate, Parker, ventured to speak again.

"May it please you, sir, they're signalling," said he.

"Let 'em signal till blazes!" replied Burke ironically; "do you think ez I'm daft enough to parley with 'em? No, I reckon not."

"They say—for I read their flags," continued the mate, disregarding his bluster—"that if you don't let them come aboard at once, they'll fire shell on you."

"They say that, do they?" cried the skipper with heat; "well, I guess I ain't a dictionary, but I've got a word to answer that. Clear the aft gun there!"

The men ran aft at his word and cleared the Nordenfelt gun, seeming to find a great consolation in the work. There was not one among them that had yet seen an action, either afloat or ashore; and to such as these the fire from the *Nero*—for they now knew the name of the cruiser—was a terror which the excitement of reply alone could mitigate. Even the Scotchman breathed a breath of enthusiasm, and stood near the group of workers, shouting and gesticulating with an energy altogether foreign to his countrymen. And he was in the very throes of a wild speech of exhortation when the *Nero* fired, for the second time, as she rose upon a great wave, and her shell, striking the yacht abaft the engine-room, but well above the water-line, carried away the bulwarks and shivered the skylight of the saloon into countless atoms. For long moments after the loud report a cloud of thick choking smoke held down upon the deck of the yacht, but when it cleared away three men lay dead of those about the gun; and the Scotchman was not to be seen. He had stood at the very point of contact, and the bursting shell had blown his body into the sea.

When the whole havoc following this—in one

sense—lucky shot was to be reckoned, the fear of the crew passed quickly to wild rage. Men, roaring like beasts, began to work the Nordenfelt wildly; or shook their fists in savage fury; or begged for liquor in the moments when reaction brought a new terror. The very deck they worked on was all slippery with foam and wet, making passage difficult; and the splinters of the broken woodwork, splashed with the blood of the dead, washed about in little pools near the scuppers.

As for the poor fellows who had gone down, they let them lie where they fell, their eyes looking up with a glassy and rigid gaze to the heaven they could not see; their bodies rolling with the way of the ship, or even being trodden upon by the maddened brutes over whom the pall of capture loomed so threateningly. All this time the bellowing of Burke upon the bridge was scarcely audible in the shriek of the wind, which seemed to gather new strength from its momentary rest. The scattered billows of cloud were now bound together by the hurricane in an arc of dense blackness, whence the rain descended, and whipped the faces of the men until both they and those upon the cruiser abandoned all attempts at further exchange of shell and shot, and went onward to the horizon of blackness and the very depths of the hurricane.

In this mutual truce before a greater power than man's, the pursuit was held until two bells, at which time the *Semiramis* crossed the mouth of the

English Channel, still running southward, having sighted the White Star liner *Teutonic*, outward bound; and, at a later hour, the Cunarder *Campania*, making for Queenstown. Both ships plunged into the huge seas in a way that betokened the strength of the west wind, and cast fountains of foaming spray from their prows as they were swept by the green water which seemed to mount almost to their hurricane decks. But they exchanged signals with the *Nero*, and when Messenger saw it he said—

"Burke, that's bad; we shall have a whole fleet at our heels in twenty-four hours."

"Maybe," said Burke; "but I dun know ez worse luck'll come of it. That ship yonder is the last thing the Britishers have done, or she'd never have kept her mark on me all these hours, I guess."

"Wal, we've got to thank this handsome zephyr for something," interposed Kenner, who had been immovable at the door of the chart-room after he had come upon the bridge; "if it hadn't blown wild cats since yesternight, I reckon there'd have been a swimming party."

"We'll fix it up yet, if there's no more ideas amongst us than we've got now," said Messenger gloomily; but Burke took him up quickly, crying—

"I guess not. If there's eyes left in my head, she's tailing off. Which among you is bearing me witness?"

"Tailing off!" yelled Kenner. "Do you say so? God forgive you, I believe you're right!"

"He is right," said Messenger. "She's half a mile further off than she was an hour ago."

It is an old remark that, in moments of great danger, the least oscillation in the balance of fortune is construed by those whom it favours as a great victory. No sooner did the crew hear Burke's words than they shouted with a savage joy, which was as repulsive as their raving of an hour ago. Crowding upon the poop, with a curse upon rule, they roared out wild defiance and brutal oaths, as though the wind would bear them to the distant vessel. Then, when they had run a signal upon the flag-halyards, they lowered it and hoisted it to express their merriment; and a brute exceeding the others in brutality, suggesting that they should show their dead, they triced up one of the bodies to the gaff and allowed it to swing in hideous mockery.

Through all this Burke was silent.

"They're letting the steam go," said he; "and if you don't want a scald, leave 'em be."

Meanwhile the fact that the yacht was distancing the *Nero* was indisputable. She must have been then three miles from her, and it seemed possible that before night she would have run right out of sight.

To Messenger the time looked more than opportune for the shoot from the shore; but Burke enlightened him with one of those surprises which he appeared to gloat upon.

"You're a mighty smart talker ashore, Prince," said he; "but you ain't worth a dollar a month, let alone a dime, at this business. Do you think ez I'm going to shift for Monte Video with the matter of a hundred ton of coal aboard?"

"Then what are you going to do?" asked Messenger, a new fear seizing him.

"I'm going to coal at Corunna in Spain; and this fall of wind is going to help me."

"But you loaded up with enough for the passage," cried Messenger; "that was all arranged."

"At sixteen knots," answered Burke grimly, "not at twenty-two, d'ye see? And you've been having twenty-two since the middle of last night."

"I never thought of that," said the other. "It's one of the things I didn't take in."

"I should fancy not," said Burke. "We ain't all so clever, though our tongues is long. But you've got to think of it now."

"It's a bad business, any way," replied the Prince; and then, for the first time since he had come aboard, his face clouded, and he did not seem to hear what was said to him.

CHAPTER IX.

THE TRAGEDY OF THE FLIGHT.

THE rumour that the *Semiramis* had not coal enough on board her to make the passage to the south was quick to be spread abroad amongst the hands; and it did not fail to inspire them for a moment with those gloomy thoughts which had already come upon Messenger. It was obvious to the meanest intelligence that danger lay near any European shore, and that safety was to be had only in the freer atmosphere of South American republics, where writs travel in shackles and treaties of extradition are mostly matters for mockery. Once in sight of Monte-Video, every man would have breathed a new breath of hope and of enterprise; but cooped up in a small yacht, with one of the fastest cruisers floating at their heels, and the necessity before them of touching at a Spanish port, what anticipation of ultimate success could the best among them entertain?

While the crew had thus a momentary appreciation of the position, the fact that they were rapidly leaving the *Nero* behind acted as a tonic upon their spirits and presently recalled them to joviality. All that afternoon, as the cruiser's hull sank upon the horizon, they sang merrily; and when Burke, to save coal, reduced speed that there might be no doubt of the bunkers holding out to Corunna, there was almost the suspicion of riotous freedom amongst them. Such a display of spirits endured well into the night, the gale falling away somewhat after eight bells, and the moon flooding picturesquely upon the wildness of the Bay; but all were weary with the long watching, and at midnight the hands turned in, and the others made no delay in following their example, leaving Kenner as sentinel at the door and the ever humble Parker in his place upon the bridge. And for some time these men had nothing to do but to listen to the song of the gale and the wash of the sea, or to take a frequent look away to the shadowed horizon where the pursuing cruiser lay, though not plain to their sight.

Now, Kenner, as the earlier record shows, was, in spite of his ever-ready braggadocio, a superstitious man. He had gone through the whole of this adventure with the feeling that ill to him personally was like to come of it; and on this particular evening his fears gripped him incessantly. For one thing, he could not rest assured that the *Nero* was really outpaced, and he went often to the deck to ask of Parker if there was any sign of her on the near sea, or show of her lights which would allow an estimate of the distance between them. But Parker invariably assured him that it was all right—" perfectly right, sir"—and he went back to the book he could not read and the cigar which he did not care to smoke. Towards six bells in the middle watch his uneasiness became as profound as Fisher's had been some nights gone, and he even went the length of waking Messenger, who started up at once and felt for his pistol, expecting to hear of a new trouble with the men, or of anticipation of it.

"Well, what is it?" said he, when he had blinked awhile in the light. "What's the matter with you?"

"That's what I'm asking myself," said Kenner. "I've got as many jumps as a colt in a corral."

"You?"

"Yes, me!" replied Kenner. "I've not a strong love for nights. I've shot men, you'll remember, and it ain't particular pleasant to hear 'em talking. The sea's full of 'em to-night; I can see 'em every way I turn!"

Messenger shrugged his shoulders.

"That comes of having an imagination; it's a dangerous thing to cultivate recollections. I'll have to sit up with you; or, better still, you'll have to go to bed."

"I think not," said Kenner. "I guess I'd want a draught stronger than any medicine man could give me to sleep to-night. I'm going to see it through, if it's a week."

"It won't be that," answered Messenger shortly; "to-morrow should pretty well settle it. But let's get above and learn what's stirring"

They went on deck to find a night of weighty darkness, and no show of a single ship's light anywhere upon the horizon. The sea was still very rough; but the combat of fierce breakers had in part given way to a long swell which followed the fall of the hurricane; and the steady roll of the ship was welcome after the constant lurching which they had known for some days. Indeed, there was great vigour in the cold of the night air; and the flecks of surf which the wind scattered in their faces brought a freshness and a sense of strength which can only be had afloat and in the teeth of an ocean wind. Kenner especially got courage when he had escaped the close atmosphere of the saloon; and, as he lighted a fresh cigar, he bawled up to the bridge where Parker was, and asked, for the tenth time, "What news?"

"There's no change, if it please you, gentlemen," said the meek Parker.

"Was there any sight of the ship when the wind fell?" asked Kenner.

"Not a sight, gentlemen," replied Parker. "I hope I do my duty, gentlemen; I try to—indeed I do, gentlemen; and if it depends upon me, there'll be no danger—not the least, I assure you."

"What does the tachometer show now?" inquired Messenger.

"It shows sixteen knots, I believe; I may say with confidence, sixteen knots and a fraction which can scarcely be of moment."

"Isn't it rather dangerous to keep it down to that with dark about us like this?" asked Messenger, who had been looking aft over the port quarter for some time.

"That's what I told the skipper; but I may say without any offence that he is short, very short, gentlemen," answered Parker apologetically.

"What did he say when you told him?" interposed Kenner.

"Really, sir, I could not venture to repeat the words—so short, so very short."

"That's Burke all over," said Kenner; "he'd swear away his own head for the sake of getting an oath off. I'd quicken up a bit, if I were you, and take his warm language on a thick hide. I guess I don't like the look of it at all, eh, Prince?"

"I haven't liked the look of it for twenty hours past," replied Messenger, as the wind scattered fire from his cigar, and it went away glowing to leeward. "If I were Parker I'd put her at twenty knots, and let him ramp; but it's not my business, as I said before. Have a cigar, Parker?"

"Well, gentlemen," said the mate unctuously, "you are very kind; and I'm sure I hope you're satisfied with me. I'll ring down for twenty knots if you wish it; but he'll be very angry when the watch changes."

"Refer him to me," said Messenger, taking Kenner's arm; and then they walked aft, where the tarpaulin covered the damaged skylight, and getting what shelter they could from wind and spray, they continued the conversation.

"I may be thick, Prince," said Kenner, "but I'm blessed if I can realise that we're afloat on this job."

"If you've any doubts," answered Messenger, "you'd better go and wash in the money downstairs."

"Ay, it's there right enough," continued Kenner, "though a man's got to be good at figgers to know what's the meaning of a million sterling, even in dollars—by thunder! To think that you and I closed on it from a bit of a talk with a kid at Monaco!"

"Three months ago exactly," said Messenger, "and not a week since I told you that my plans were perfect. Well, there's always a rift in a lute like this, and you've got to mend it before you've any music. My mistake was a small one comparatively, but its effects have been wide. I've no doubt whatever that the mate was picked up, and that this business is written about in London now with letters as big as your foot—and that's pretty big, Kenner."

"I can't think why on earth you took the chap aboard," said Kenner thoughtfully; "I'd have seen him stretched first."

"Exactly; it's amazing how many things you think of when they can't possibly be of any use to anyone. I had my doubts about him, it is true, and was weak enough to take another man's estimate of them. That's where the folly came in."

"There," replied Kenner, "I'm with you all along; a big project means a big mind, and only one.

We've had too many heads in this since the start of it, and what's the result? Why, we're on the road to be straightened out, every one of us. Look at it any way you like, you can't bluff it, for the hand ain't good enough. And I've had the notion ringing in my head ever since last night, when I dreamed we were under."

"Look here!" said Messenger angrily, "don't let us have that woman's nonsense again. I can't see that the danger's insurmountable. It's great, of course; but we'll have to go into Corunna under a false name for coal, and then to risk it through the Doldrums. I should call the chance an even one."

Kenner had more words to say; but he stopped of a sudden as a figure joined them by the skylight, and he saw that it was the figure of Fisher.

"Hello, young 'un!" cried he, "what brings you crawling out of bed?"

"I can't sleep," said Fisher; "I've done nothing but dream ridiculously ever since I turned in."

"You've caught it from Kenner," interposed Messenger, a little contemptuously; "he's had a mountain on his chest for three days past."

"I dreamt the cruiser had picked us up, and we were hit," said Fisher; "in fact, I saw the water rushing into my cabin, and it wasn't until I got on deck here that I knew I'd made a fool of myself."

"Wait a bit," said Kenner, "I guess you needn't be so ready—look there!"

As he spoke the three men who had been standing in darkness, were held to their places with cries upon their lips as a great flood of focussed light poured upon the deck of the yacht, and gave illumination for the tragedy which was to come. It was the search-light of the cruiser flashing upon them, and as they stood and a great shout burst from them, they saw that she was not half a mile distant. Then flame shot from her gun amidships, and, with a terrible piercing crash, the yacht rolled her lee scuppers under.

For some moments a deadly stillness followed the sickening shiver of steel and of woodwork; but it was a stillness of terror and foreboding. The screws of the yacht had ceased to work; steam poured up in fleecy hissing volumes from her engine-room; failing to head the waves, she was washed by the swell until she lay a heavy, rolling mass deep down in the sea. As for the hands, they had come up almost with the reverberation of the shot, and stood—many of them half-naked—dumb with the terror of the scene and its development. All was now still below, where dreadful cries had been heard for a moment after the shot fell; the smitten ship rolled heavily to starboard, flooded with spray and water; her desperate plunges foretold beyond questioning that the end of it all was near.

At this time it did not appear possible that the *Semiramis* could float for an hour. Although the cruiser ceased to fire at her, and lay playing upon her with the spreading radiance of her magnificent light, every man on deck awaited the moment when his body should shrink under the cold touch of the sea and he should be drawn down in the vortex at once to death and to burial.

This very uncertainty, and the fact that the yacht continued to float in the face of her sore plight, added pitiably to the sufferings of the men. Burke had staggered upon deck at the first shock, and now stood muttering upon the bridge, unable to gather his wits for a coherent order. The others, holding for shelter to the safety-line rigged aft, neither spoke nor thought of aught but the near prospect of death. Again, as in the other crisis, it was the voice of the one-legged man, Joe, who brought them all to their senses.

"Be gor, gemmelen," cried he, stumping aft with a quick step, "you go for blazes, sahs, and no mistake; you get your next slops mighty hot, sahs; you all go in the devil's foretop, and sign for long time, gemmelen—oh yes, be gor!"

He stumped away, and shouted, now mocking, now inciting the crew to action, until even Burke was aroused at his words.

"You there!" cried he to a small group of lascars and of seamen huddled up near the windlass. "Where's Nicolini?"

Nicolini was the engineer, but he and his "second" lay dead in the engine-room; and when no one answered Burke, the skipper turned to Parker—

"Don't stand shivering like a calf!" he roared,

"sound her for'ard, and see where she's hit; and aft there, strip that gun and see if there's shot that's dry."

They bustled up at his orders, and, although the ship lay heavy in the trough of the seas, they began to work both the Nordenfelt guns, and to shoot with small hope of effect at the cruiser, which was now preparing to get a boat from the davits and to board the yacht before she sank. So clear was this that the near proximity of the new danger of capture drove, for a moment, all thought of the other danger from the men's minds; and they looked about them for weapons, with fierce threats upon their lips. Anon, they observed that the lifeboat had actually been launched, and they beheld her coming towards them, the great arc of light illuminating her path, and showing her, now thrown high upon a mount of water, now cast deep into the fallow of the sea; and the discovery moved them even to a greater intensity of savage anger. Yet this would have availed them no more than their loud defiance had not a very curious turn of fortune befriended them, and for the hour, at any rate, diverted all the peril of this intrepid attack.

The chance came when the *Nero's* boat was almost upon them. How it was brought to pass they could realise; but of a sudden the light of the cruiser, which had begun to follow its boat, went out, and left blackness upon the sea. Scarcely daring to speak or to hope, the men of the *Semiramis* waited to hear the coming of the boat, but it never came. Twice the cruiser fired a gun, but no shell hissed over them; and when a third gun was fired, after an interval, they were sure that it was a signal of recall to the boat. Then, indeed, an expectation of safety, newer, stronger, more potent, led them from their cowering *laissez-aller;* and, as Burke roared the order for the hand-pumps to be worked, and for new soundings to be made, a ray even of cheerfulness moved them to activity.

At the end of half an hour, during which time they waited in momentary expectation of seeing the search-light again, dawn began to break upon the sea, being the morning of the fifth day. The first thought of all the men was for the cruiser, but when the night lifted they saw her a long way off on their port bow, and no smoke came from her funnels, nor did she appear to contemplate any further pursuit. At the end of an hour she had almost disappeared, and Burke called a conference in the cabin; but the hands worked unceasingly to pump out the engine-room, and they set upon the two short masts every stitch of canvas they would bear.

Burke's views were simple.

"We're knocked fair and square," said he, "with a hole big ez a barn door. From what I've learned, we can't look to mend it this side of Spain."

"Will the yacht float that long?" asked Kenner, when he had heard the opinion.

"Maybe; maybe not," said Burke; "but the sea's fallin' and there's the boats."

"Wal," said Kenner, "I don't see where the boats come in—leastways, not if you're going to take the yaller load along."

"I am still asking myself," interposed Messenger, "why they let us go at the very moment they were on top of us."

"You've to inquire down in their engine-room, I guess, to larn that," said Burke. "You may bet a bottle they didn't drop it because a fly settled on 'em."

"Do you think you can make Corunna with the rags you've got?" asked Kenner.

"I can try," replied Burke; "and if it happens ez I don't—wal, you ain't much worse off than swimmin' abed here."

This was not an untrue reflection upon the condition of the saloon, into which the sea had poured until every cushion reeked of damp; and some of the kegs of gold even splashed in rolling pools of water. Everywhere below, the yacht was sodden with the sea. Although her custom was to stand up well under canvas, she now half-buried herself in the long breakers, and plunged ahead with heavy shocks and shivering labour. To live on her became a compulsory picnic, where the food was got haphazard; and was eaten with the salt which the waves cast. Once or twice she passed ships, and signalled to them that she needed no assistance; but the men wearying in the work, became stupid with liquor, and lay about wet to the skin, or shivering with the deadly chill of exposure, which for many was to pass so soon into the chill of death. All that day and the next the stupor and inanition hung like a pall upon those who had made so great a cast for fortune, and upon their masters who had conceived it. To many of these a moment's warmth, a ray of heat, the shelter of a dry coverlet, would have been worth ten times their share of the vast plunder which now swam in the lapping seas of the saloon. But for them there was no relief. Water washed in the galley fires; the engine-room was full of it; the whole yacht reeked of it; and in the general desolation the men cried for land as children cry for the homes they have left, and the havens of their comfort.

At what time—if ever—this wretched ship would have made Corunna, no man may presume to tell. On the night of the eighth day the voyage ended abruptly, and with a mighty shock which, at the very moment of its coming, ended the yacht's history. She had struck hard upon the rocks of the northern coast of Spain; and, as the seas rolled over her, and the men screamed in their terror, the commanding voice of Burke was heard crying—

"Shorewards, if you'd live! and every man for himself!"

"'SHOREWARDS, IF YOU'D LIVE!'" (p. 112).

CHAPTER X.

INTO THE UNKNOWN HAVEN.

BURKE'S cry rang out above the thunder of the surf, and echoed through the ship to its ultimate depths. Men in the first grip of sleep sprang from their resting-places at its clarion note, only to find themselves dashed hither and thither as splinters in a whirlpool. Others, dumb to knowledge in the clutch of drink, were drowned as they lay; or washed, yet insensible, to the crags and spikes of the hidden reef, where death took them. A few clung to safety-lines, or lashed themselves to booms or shrouds, and thus, for a spell, bore the brunt of the breaking seas.

The intensity of the night was so profound that for a long while no man knew where the ship lay or what was her environment. In that hour the zenith of the heaven was marked by an envelope of inky vapour, which hid the moon and the stars; and the chilling rain beat incessantly upon those who for many days had cried for warmth and had not found it. As for the sea itself, it rose and fell with thunderous echoes. The gigantic breakers, driven by the north-west wind in hollowed and o'er-toppling ridges of water dissolved themselves at length upon the

H

reef in swirling eddies of foam, or played with fountains of silver spray upon the darkness of the night; or rushed fiercely with torrent force between the channels of the crags. And over all was the trembling voice of the tempest—a voice which seemed to quaver with the cries of the sea's spirits and to join in one piteous and longdrawn wail the lamentations of the heavens and the dirge of the deep.

When the first shock had struck the yacht, Messenger, Kenner, and Fisher had been in the saloon, wrapped in blankets, and seeking sleep, even in face of the omnivorous damp. They had given over, for some hours, any thought of the gold, since the mockery of its possession was too ostensible in the presence of the overwhelming peril of the sea; and other questions—but principally the one, shall we see the shore again?—were upon their minds, to the exclusion of all else. Thus it came that they lay in wakefulness when the *Semiramis* plunged onward to the iron haven of inhospitable Galicia; and struck, at last, some miles eastward of the terrible Cabo Ortegal. But at the first touch of the shock the men awoke, and, springing to their feet in the infinite darkness, found themselves battling with a flood of water which poured upon the cabin and threatened to end them as they stood.

As they stood, half-choking, Fisher's voice was the first to be heard.

"Prince!" cried he, "Prince! where are you! My God, what is it?"

"I'm here," cried Messenger back to him; "give me your hand. Did you feel the ship strike? Where's Kenner?"

"Going under," moaned Kenner, with water in his throat.

"Then make for the ladder," cried Messenger, as he exerted himself with a supreme effort. "Hal, hold to me. If we've no legs now, we'll drown like dogs."

And he fell to calling "Burke! Burke!" as though the skipper could hear him above the crash of seas.

For a spell the struggle was fierce; but Fisher, who had his courage back, fighting water with all his nerve, grasped the companion at last, and hauled himself up and the man with him. But the American, tumbling headlong on the slippery floor, fell at the foot of the stairs, and lay there, while another sea poured its suffocating crest upon him. And there would have been his end but for the lad who, coming upon the deck, immediately looked about him to see how his companions had fared.

"Where's Kenner?" he asked; adding, "I thought he was with you."

"He is on the floor, and dead by this," gasped the other, as the water cut his face, and he clung, with hands benumbed and shivering limbs, to the rail of the poop; "but it's every man for himself now! What an end! My God, what an end!"

He said this, hoping to hold back Fisher, who had turned to the companion again, for it came to him that he would be better wanting the American's company. But the lad has not heard the words, and was at the ladder while the man yet spoke them.

When at last he brought himself into the saloon, the rollers still shot water through the sky-light, and much poured through the open hatchway; the whole bulk of it washing dismally from end to end of the cabin as the hull swayed even in the shelter of the rocky cup which held it. Utter darkness, too, was upon the place! and when the lad stood shivering at the foot of the companion, he hesitated for a moment before leaving even the comparative light of the open. But the mood passed, and with a deep breath he stepped into the saloon; and being almost immediately thrown off his foothold, his head went under the water, and he fought again with the unspeakable terror of the danger and the darkness.

Now, indeed, the water surged in his eyes, and got into his gullet, so that he gasped for breath like one upon the point of suffocation. Then he stood again, with the flood almost at his waist, and going to advance a step, he struck his head against the frieze of the ceiling, and was thrown back almost insensible upon the soaking cushions. But the fall saved Kenner. As he lurched back with the pain of the blow, he put his foot upon the body of the American, and in a moment he had him in his arms and was staggering towards the companion. Nor did he know until he had laid him upon the deck, and there made sure that he breathed, whether the man were alive or dead.

The amazing darkness was, plainly, the first cause of so few escaping from the yacht. As the three men lay in what shelter they could, and their cries were unheard in the play of seas, they had no vision or sign of that which had happened forward. And such a sight would have been of little moment to Kenner, who was nigh insensible; but the others had terror in the thought that they were alone, and yearned for a sight of the sky as sick men weary for dawn. Again and again Fisher asked of Messenger, "Can you see anything?" Again and again he got for answer the plain monosyllable "No." Once he thought that he observed the figure of Burke, black upon the bridge, and heard his strong voice even above the crying of the gale; but the vision was gone in a moment, and the face of the impenetrable night alone remained. And for more than an hour the three survivors, as they then thought themselves, clung together for warmth under the poor breakwater they had found, and waited only for the death that seemed about to come upon them.

It must have been three o'clock, and very near to the hour of dawn, when there was a break in the enveloping vapour, and less thunder of the waves. At that time, the three men, lying in dull stupor, heard the sound of Burke's voice—unmistakable and clear—and were by it aroused to show of activity. For the cleavage of cloud cast a dim light upon the scene, and showed to them the huge form of the man of iron upon the bridge; and the deep baying of his voice was to be heard above the falling seas.

"You there, forward!" he bellowed, "that mast's going—look to yourselves!"

He spoke almost with the spreading of the steely light, then striking cold and grey upon the turmoil of the sea and upon the ship. The passing of the deeper darkness had with far-reaching swiftness conjured—as it seemed, from the very deep—distant shapes and forms as of cliff and headland; had set down a line of foam-washed shore; had surrounded the yacht with jagged spires of iron rock, which stood over her as grim sentinels. The land rose a mile away dark and terrible and precipitous; but a great gulf of churning, seething billows cut them from it; and as the men realised their position, a great shout went up from them, a-wailing and a-cursing as of men about to die, but for whom in death there was no sleep.

"The mast! Come off the mast, I tell you!" roared Burke for the second time, and the men aft took up the cry as they saw his meaning. Eight of the hands were huddled together in the foretop; and the mast which sheltered them was giving to the seas, and threatening with every shock to plunge into the cavern of spuming water which lay between the crags.

In this minute of panic one of the hands, bolder than his fellows, set off to swarm across the topmast stay, and was then hanging in mid-air, while the others watched him, but made no move to dare the passage. At first it appeared probable that the foremast would go before he had reached the bridge and had dropped upon it; and the intense excitement of those watching him got strength from the lurches of the stay, which promised every moment to hurl the seaman from his hold. Nor did those aft understand why the men remained in the foretop, wanting the knowledge that the yacht had broken in half at the engine room, and that her forepart lay completely submerged; while there was another great channel running between the aft-deck and the poop. The eight hands had taken refuge in the foretop at the first crash of disaster; and when the light came, they were, for the more part, half-dead with the cold and incapable of effort. One alone amongst them had life for the passage of the stay, and his struggles were unavailing, as the sequel proved.

The fellow had nigh reached the bridge—was getting purchase to make the leap, in fact—when the scene culminated. A "ninth" wave hit the tottering mast, and it snapped like a rotten branch, dashing the seven men hard upon the surface of the sea, and throwing the eighth from his hold so that he went down as from a trapeze. Then his head struck a spike of rock with such a horrid sound that those who heard it covered their faces and turned from the sight. Of the seven who went under with the mast but two rose again, showing terror-struck visages in the dawn light, and crying piteously, as though the sea would relent or the rocks rise up to give them foothold.

Meanwhile, Burke upon the bridge paced like a caged beast, for there was water everywhere below him, and no prospect of passage by which he might reach the safer haven of the poop. But when he saw the three aft, he seemed to gather coherence, and he bawled to them—

"You there, have you got ever a line?"

"Not a yard but the lashing," roared Messenger in reply.

"Do you make out anything ashore?" he asked next.

"Nothing but a headland, and hills beyond it," cried Messenger; but he went on with a question—

"Is it ebb or flow?"

"It's ebb, if I'm not dreaming," roared Burke. "We struck at the top of the tide. Is your end holding, or is she full?"

"She's holding; but there's more shift in her than I like," responded Messenger.

"Same ez with me," yelled Burke. "I'm going shorewards. I'll die quick, by gosh! if there ain't no other road."

The man was calm enough, and they watched him grasp a belt from the bridge and worm his shoulders into it. He stood thus irresolute above the chasm of waters for a long-drawn minute, and spoke again before the sea cast him to the venture, not biding his irresolution—

"Where's Kenner?" said he.

"Dying," gasped Kenner, who had got consciousness, and sat up against the hatchway; but his croaking voice was lost in the scream of wind.

"Is he gone?" shouted the skipper, pausing at the leeside of the bridge.

"No, but he's mighty sick," cried Messenger, helping his voice with his hands.

"Wal," responded Burke, "he's had a run for his money, anyway. We'll share the yaller load in hell, all of us, I guess."

He was about to say more, but the bridge beneath him of a sudden fell before the ceaseless onslaught of the swell, and, rearing up its edge high above the water, disappeared in a moment, carried by the rushing current which swept between the crags. Those on the poop saw Burke battling with the surf for a spell; then he disappeared between the islets of rock, and before they could think more of him their attention was turned to their own position and the hazardous shifting of the stern of the yacht.

Fisher was the first to notice it.

"Prince," said he, "we've got to follow him—the poop's going over."

"I was noticing it," replied Messenger.

"Do you think you could swim to shore if you got free of the rocks?" asked Fisher, adding, "one of us will have to stand by Kenner."

Messenger turned to look at the American, who was sitting half-dazed and voiceless, and he said—

"Kenner, we're going to swim for it."

At these words the American raised his head and struggled to his feet.

"You won't leave me," he gasped; "I can't die alone!" And then he fell to wailing like a woman; and staggered toward the door of the staircase, whence he slid down the inclined plane of the deck until he was caught by the stream amidships and carried into the whirlpool. Fisher had followed him instinctively, and was in the water to grip him even before he sank for the first time; and from that moment it was the venture of life against the cataracts of the reef. "Twice," said the lad, in his account of it, "I felt the seas closing over my head. Then a great hill of wave rose over me, and sent me deep down with a terrible singing in my ears. Each time that I rose, holding to Kenner—who, to my surprise, did not hamper me in the water—I saw the rocky pinnacles towering (they looked a great way) above me; and I was drawn so near to them in the vortex that I thought every minute I should be ended with a clout on the head which would stun me. How it really was I cannot say, but suddenly, as Kenner began to give in, and I was wasting all my strength in holding him, we were carried immediately into a channel where there was scarcely any sea; and from that moment I could swim in comfort. Even then there seemed no hope of reaching the dark line of the shore; and the great headland, which loomed like some black phantom on my right hand, appeared only as a shadow on my hopes. You may judge of my surprise at last, when, having swum no more than a couple of hundred yards, I found myself able to touch ground with my feet, and discovered that there was not a man's height of water below me. Thence onward was lurching, staggering work, but half an hour of it brought us right up out of the sea, and we sank breathless upon a heap of sand at the foot of a tremendous cliff, and there lay like dead men."

Meanwhile Messenger had not hesitated to face the terror of the rock-pool, and, having given one piteous glance at the wreck wherein all his hope lay, had dived boldly from the poop; and had come more readily than the others into the comparative calm of the open water, and so to the shallows. He was, as were the two who had first reached land, exhausted and nigh dead; he trembled with the cold; his face was an ashen colour; his clothes hung in rags upon him. But his first act on coming to the inhospitable haven was to turn a long look to the distant islets, where the relic of the ship lay, and to stand motionless for many minutes before he sank upon the sand and felt that the life was going out of him.

And he knew in that moment that the great stake he had played for was lost, and that the gold was gone.

CHAPTER XI.

ON THE FIELD OF THE AFTER-MATH.

DAY broke with southern maturity, a day of relentless sun and intermittent breeze; and the warmth was as wine to the men marooned by the act of God in the haven of Galicia. Even Kenner, who had been very near to death, felt the blood coursing through his veins again; and Fisher slept upon a sheet of sand, unmindful of the powerful rays which poured down upon him even in the hours of the early morning. Messenger alone, shivering and silent, was cowed into the depths of melancholy by the overwhelming visitation which had fallen upon the yacht.

Nor, indeed, is it to be marvelled at that this man, to whose far-reaching mind the whole emprise had been due, should have lain under such subjection. Even three days before the coming of that unlooked-for disaster, a future, at least of action and of possibility, opened before him. The possession of the gold in the cabin of the yacht had steeled him to face all the hazards of exile, of capture, and of pursuit. He contemplated, with no dismay, the vigilance of governments and the zeal of private persons. Once in

South America with some hundreds of thousands of pounds at his call, and his own wits to befriend him, he would have scoffed alike at the diplomacy of ministers and the corruptibility of republics. But on that morning after the wreck he stood on the shores of Spain, a hunted man and a man without resource, friendless in an unbefriending land, the wreck of an ambition, and the tool of a crime: and, as the gloom of his hope deepened, his face had more than its usual pallor, his mind was limp, his marvellous foresight seemed entirely to have left him.

Kenner, it may be, would have known the depressing spell of thoughts such as these if the buffeting he had got in the seas had not knocked thought out of him and left to him only thankfulness that he was rid of the peril. But Fisher, who had passed through the week as a man in a dream, had neither hurt from the sea nor a haunting of the mind to combat; and he slept, being content that he had come to shore and that the terrible days of the voyage were gone for ever.

The place where they had come to was rugged enough, yet by no means lacking the picturesque. From the headland of rock which marked the extent of a mountainous and black peninsula, the shore trended rapidly into a gentle bay. At the head of this there came tumbling down a narrow sparkling river, which flowed out of the hills so steeply that its falls and tiny cataracts were discernible from the remoter shore whereon the castaways had been thrown.

In this bay, whose beach was of a curiously gold-like sand, irradiating flashing lights in the play of the sun, the sea lay with little movement, tiny waves lapping the shore gently, as with caresses; and the softest of breezes coming from the land, laden with the scent of flowers and of the hay. It is true that the scene derived little ornament from its background of wild, seemingly inaccessible, and treeless hills; but in the lower valleys there was almost a wealth of verdure, and a venta or church perched here and there amongst the heights (but at a great way from the shore), was evidence of some human presence; though there was none near the sea nor at the place where the men of the *Semiramis* had first touched land.

There all was bleak and barren; the walls of iron rock shot up with forbidding face to vast heights; there was no sign of track or path, of coastguard or signal-station; and away out to sea the needles of rocks whereon the yacht had foundered seemed alone in possession of the water. Beyond them and the line of sandy shallow the great rollers of the bay sported and foamed in long lines of green and white, and cast up fountains of glistening spray above the place of wreckage and the fateful reef. And all in all, it was a scene of desolation, and one which warranted the dumb despair of Messenger and his friend, and even the sleep of the weary lad.

Fisher, perhaps, would have lain all day had not Kenner, coming to some sense with the sun, aroused him before nine o'clock and pointed out the danger of his proceeding.

"I'll tell you what, youngster," said he, as the boy opened his eyes drowsily, "you aren't in Hyde Park, and this doesn't strike me as a particularly choice spot for camping. You'd got the sun full down on you."

"I must have had," said Fisher, rubbing his head woefully. "I feel as heavy as lead. Where's the Prince?"

Messenger rose at his words and came across to them.

"That's just what I'm asking myself," said he as he sat down beside them, hatless as they were, and half-dressed, since most of his clothes were spread upon the beach to dry. "Where are we, and where are the rest of them?"

"Do you think that any of them lived besides ourselves?" asked Fisher earnestly.

"Lived!" said Kenner contemptuously; "how could they? By gosh! boy, if it hadn't been for you, Jake Kenner would be breakfasting wrong side up this morning."

"Anyway," cried Fisher, "you'd have done the same for me."

The American went a little red in the face at this, for he knew that, had the positions and the power been reversed, Fisher would have gone down like a stone; but he checked his thought and, holding out his hand, said simply—

"Shake, and, if I live, look to me to stand by you. I wouldn't go through that night again not to get the gold back."

At the word "gold," Fisher turned sympathetically to Messenger, and asked—

"Is some of the loss yours, Prince?"

"Yes," said Messenger with a shrug; "Kenner and I are the chief sufferers."

"Won't some of the kegs wash ashore?" said Fisher next.

"I think not," replied Messenger, smiling for the first time. "Gold is a little heavier than flax, eh, Kenner?"

"I can't talk of it," said Kenner, turning away with the sigh of a broken man. "Every time I look away there, it's like putting a knife in me. What an end!"

"It won't bear words," interposed Messenger suddenly; and then, without more talk, he began to pace the beach with long strides, pausing often to look seawards, or to bite at his finger-nails, as his habit was.

"He's thinking something out, I guess," said Kenner as he watched him. "What he thinks out has generally got grit at the bottom of it."

"I wish he'd think out breakfast," said Fisher. "I don't know how you feel, but I've a void; and there doesn't seem much to eat here but cold rock and seaweed."

"I've been of your opinion since you set me down,"

said Kenner feelingly; "I'd give a pound for a jug of wine."

"It would be the same thing if you'd give two," cried Fisher; "that is, if we stop here."

"If we stop here," cried Kenner. "Wal, I'm fixed up, any road. I couldn't walk a mile if a hogshead of dollars was staked on it."

"Let's begin by drying ourselves, at any rate," continued Fisher. "The mariners in Horace hung up their clothes as an offering to the gods, you know. Here goes for the complement."

He stripped himself to the waist, and, making headgear of his handkerchief, he laid out his own clothes and those of Kenner in the glaring sun, and then, getting what shade he could from the overhanging crags, he said as a man who is satisfied—

"It occurs to me, Kenner, that if you played the Barmecide, and I played Shacabac, we might pass our time until the washing is dry. It looks as though it were going to be precious slow here; and I'm just as stiff as a lay-figure."

"You may knock me down in the same lot," cried Kenner with gusto; "what I can spell right here is thirst, and stroke the t's, too!"

"The first thing to do, don't you know," said Fisher, with his half-jocular readiness, "is to strike inland for a town, or, failing a town, for a village, or, if we don't find either, why then for an inn. We've got some cash amongst us, surely, and, directly we can put our hands on an English consul, we'll make him send us home again. I'd give something to set foot in the Strand and breathe a real 'pea-soup,' wouldn't you?"

Kenner, hunching himself up till he resembled a bundle, looked at the boy out of the corner of his ill-set eyes, and then chuckled. He was thinking that a good many people in London would be glad to have acquaintance of the party just then. But he did not say anything; rather, he turned the conversation by pointing to Messenger.

"Where's he steering for?" he asked. "I never knew his double in my life; you can't chain him, and you can't set him free; he's all wires and wheels, like a calculating machine. Look at him now, striding along at six mile an hour, and holloaing at the hill to clear his lungs of salt; you'd think he'd got a patch in his head if you didn't know him."

"He's not holloaing at the hill," cried Fisher; "he calling to someone. There's a man running along the sand, and it looks like old Burke! It is, too, as I'm alive! What luck!"

On this he began to dress, with a disregard for the niceties of the toilet which was admirable; and Kenner, taking heart that another lived, stood up on his feet, and lurched along with him towards the distant men. There was now no doubt of Burke's identity, for there he was with his rolling, reckless gait, his arms bare, and his head without a hat, coming swiftly over the sands towards them; and when he paused, it was to waken the hills with the echo of his resounding hail. At last he stood with Messenger, and they could see him pointing hurriedly towards the reef where the yacht had struck or, again, to the bleak hills and the desert-like meadows. When they reached him, Kenner sank breathlessly upon the sand with the effort; but the skipper, curtly avoiding all greeting, continued his narration.

"What I've been tellin' 'em, Kenner," said he, "is ez we're only at the beginning of it. I'm not sure we're quite that fur, and I reckon the Prince is my way. The yaller stuff is under water right enough; but you're not wanting more'n decent eyes in your head to see that the aft end of the ship has been fixed right up in the cradle there, and that she's holding still. Maybe her timbers are knocked right out of her; maybe they ain't. If my judgment's worth a dollar, there's about six feet of water over the bar at low tide, and the kegs don't go for to travel far on a bottom like that. What we're wanting is a gig and a rope to begin on, and after that the dark to work in."

"Why the dark?" said Kenner, to whom night had become a terror. "Give me day, and take your dark to blazes!"

"He's quite right," said Messenger; "I've thought of that from the first. There must be some sort of coastguard here, and, once we're sighted, the thing will ring through Europe, and we'll have to listen to the music. Safety doesn't lay out on this shore here; it lays up in the hills and under what cover we can get. The same's true of the boat; we must lay hands on the first one we come to, and what's to be got ashore must be shipped and landed at the first possible moment. Where do you think we are, Burke?"

"We're not a continent off the toe of the Bay," replied Burke; "though, if you ask me to pin it on the chart for you, I don't know ez I could do within a hundred mile. The shore's foreign to me except by hearsay, and that's bad enough."

"I've heard strange things of it," said Messenger; "but there's no time to think of them now. The immediate necessity is meat and drink and, after that, cover."

"If I'm choosing, it's the drink you may order to bring on," interposed Kenner; "I'm as weak as a rabbit."

"You'll have to walk awhile, anyway," said Messenger. "There should be some path up to the heights from here, and the sooner we find a camping place, the better."

Kenner rose at this inducement, and, walking between two of them, made good way along the smooth sand, following the trend of the bay towards the distant river. They walked with moderate ease a mile or more, finding no break in the sheer face of the rock upon their right; for the headland was extraordinarily prominent and precipitous where its crags did not absolutely jut out above the beach.

Yet they could see that there was lower land towards the neck of the bay; and they were moved with such a powerful excitement, begotten of the thought that the money might in some part be recovered, that they went with light step, and that which was near to merriment. So they came to the place where the cliff began to show a less rugged and a shorter face, when of a sudden there was a rattling of rocks ahead of them, and a curious figure jumped out, as it were, from a ledge of the headland to the soft sand below.

The figure was that of a dark, weather-beaten Spaniard, a man of some age, but exceeding illclad. He carried an old musket slung across his worn and ragged zamarra; and wore sea-boots to his hips, though they spoke of much service and of decay. His sombrero was black, with velvet trimming upon a portion of it; and his beard fell deep upon his chest, and had grown over his face so that little was to be seen of him but dark and savage eyes, and ears that were outstanding beyond experience. But he displayed a surprised curiosity in the coming of the four; and stood watching them, or shooting quick glances out at the sea, as though he looked to find their ship at anchor or in difficulty.

When he had satisfied himself that they had no ship, but apparently were in like manner curious concerning his identity, he wheeled round as he had come, and disappeared in a moment behind a low bush; plunging, as it seemed, into the face of the rock.

They saw him, some minutes after, higher up on the side of the precipice; and then it was evident that he followed a path which led to the verdurous plains between the distant hills and the foreshore. Often he looked back at them, or stayed in his curiosity to see if they would follow him; but, observing that they did not, he went from their sight at last, although his path was to be traced by a peculiarly shrill whistling, which echoed across the ravine, but was not answered.

This sudden apparition did not appear to be to the liking either of Messenger or of Burke.

"Prince," said the latter, "that chap don't mean peace and goodwill, you bet. There's more like him in the hills for sartin, and just as handsome. I'm for moving on quick."

"Exactly," said Messenger; "the traditions of this part of the Bay aren't quite what you would call pleasant. Let's get on."

They moved at a brisk pace now, coming quickly to the goat path up which the Spaniard had disappeared; but, keeping the shelter of the lower bay, they struck for the river, thinking the possibility of getting some boat to be larger there; and when they had walked a mile, they fell upon a little cabin built curiously as a nest some few feet above the beach. It was no more than a shanty of wood, roofed with weed, and curiously ornamented with shells; but smoke mounted from a hole in its roof and curled up the cliff; and its door stood open, showing proofs of habitation within. The four men stopped at once before the hut, and seeing that no one was for the moment in possession, they held a consultation.

"I ain't goin' to say for sure, but it appears to me that this is the particular hotel of Goat-in-the-boots yonder," said Burke; "the first house in the city by the look of it."

"It's a dreadful-looking hole, certainly," said Messenger, putting his head in at the door, to withdraw it quickly, "and doesn't exactly smell of attar of roses—but there might be food there. What do you think, Kenner?"

"I was thinking you might find a keg of beer," said Kenner, stumping up, "and leave an I O U on the table for it."

"Exactly," cried Messenger; "but who's going in? I'd sooner face a cattle-stampede than that hole."

"Your senses is too highly developed, Prince," said Burke, bluffly; "you've never run a cargo of black cattle, I guess—why, for sure, they ain't exactly violets; but it depends on your taste."

With this he made a dive into the room, the others watching him while he rummaged, with no gentle hand, and came out again presently, laden with three bottles of a common wine and some great hunks of *pan de centeno*, the dry and unpalatable maize-bread of the Galicians. He was walking away with them, when Fisher called out—

"I say, we ought to pay something. I've got half a crown, if that will do."

Burke took the money, returned to the room, put the coin in his own pocket, and came out again.

"Now," said he, "the sooner we reach a yard of grass and lie low, the better; I don't hanker arter ovations myself—not much in summer."

A walk of a few furlongs carried them to the slope of the cliff, and, as the precipice decreased, so was the vegetation more abundant. They came at last to a point where the path rose, with broad steps, from the seashore to the wooded land above; and this they ascended, to find themselves upon a bare plain whereon rye had been grown; but there were trees green with some luxuriance beyond it; and a close-knit wood edging upon these again. It was in the wood that they finally took shelter, grouping themselves round the trunk of a chestnut-tree which had been felled; and upon this they spread their victuals for lack of table. The meal was sorry enough; but the men were long gone in fasting, and the American especially gulped down his wine with the unslakable thirst of the fever-stricken or the delirious.

"I was near dead for that," said he, with satisfaction, when he had emptied a bottle; "and it isn't exactly Château Lafitte, is it?"

"It's not bad stuff," said Messenger, partaking of it moderately; "but all these Spanish wines are poor in the north."

"What about the bread, then?" asked Fisher. "It reminds me of sawdust or mortar—I'm not sure which."

"The bread's all right," said Kenner, making pretence to eat it with satisfaction; "if our chance of getting up the kegs of yellow stuff was as good, I don't know that I'd find fault with the *menu*."

"You're waking up, Kenner," said Messenger; "that's the first sensible thing you've said. The question is, Where are we going to clap hands upon a boat? There ought to be a village, or at least an inn, somewhere within five miles; but it will take a lot of tacking to get a craft without raising the neighbourhood. Of course, two will have to stay to watch from the shore here; it would be a mad thing to lose sight of the place for a moment."

"That's sense," said Burke; "two of us make inland, two remain within a mile of here; but the two that goes hasn't got time on their hands, and shouldn't sleep over the job—leastwise, that's my notion of it."

The interesting point was not argued, for there came as he spoke a sharp report from the shore; and while they yet listened, the first report was followed by a second and a third, which echoed in the distant hills and sent the birds screaming from the trees.

"Do you hear that?" cried Burke. "That ain't no Spanish rat-piece, I'd lay my life on it—that's a Winchester, and I guess we're moving."

They all sprang to their feet at his words; and, keeping to the shelter of the wood, made their way quickly that they might get a sight of the shore.

CHAPTER XII.

THE FIRST OF THE SPANIARDS.

As the men followed the woodland path through a tortuous maze of abundant trees and heavy undergrowth, they came presently to a clearing on the summit of a low cliff; and when they had climbed a sharp bank, set about with thorny bushes, they found themselves upon a small plateau whence could be seen the whole sweep of the bight. Below them were the golden sand and the lapping wavelets. The turrets and spires of a castellated building shone in the sun at the far side of the bay; the murmur of the mountain stream was in their ears as it fell from ravine to ravine and bubbled at last in the blue water of the Atlantic. But vastly more engrossing than all these was the scene upon the foreshore not a quarter of a mile away from the spot on which they stood.

Here they observed at the first glance the form of the yacht's longboat drawn up in some part out of the sea, but yet the centre of a very pretty adventure. In the stern of the boat was the man called One-legged Joe, who lay back at his ease, his whole leg dangling over the side of his ship, and his leg of wood stuck up in the air with a yellow signal flag flying at the foot of it. But this display of subtle humour was not the better part of his occupation; for, as he reclined in the boat, he discharged his Winchester at intervals, and he had for targets two ragged Spaniards, who were armed only with sticks, and a third, who was no other than "Goat-in-the-boots" of the morning. The latter held his musket, and was, when Burke first saw him, loading with great haste for a renewal of the attack upon the nigger; but his fellows lay prone upon the sand in the endeavour to avoid the skim of the bullets, and were crawling slowly towards the longboat when the campers first came out upon the cliff.

Now, when Burke and his three got a sight of this, in one way, droll business, their surprise was as great as though they had seen a dead man walk up suddenly out of the sea. They had never looked to hope that any man was saved from the ship; and the amazing appearance of the cook was quite beyond their explanation. And for a breathing-space they stood, not knowing whether to laugh or to shout, while the bullets from the half-caste's rifle kicked up trails in the wet sand, and the shots from the Spaniard's musket ricochetted in the little lakes of water and appeared to cover the Englishman with spray.

"You may lay me out," said Burke, when he had surveyed the scene for some minutes, marvelling, "if that black and white nigger ain't got the life of a cat."

"I'd like to bet he's lined through with cork," muttered Kenner, as he watched him. "I never knew his like yet—and ashore in the longboat, too!"

"I saw the boat go," said Messenger, shading his eyes to be more sure with them; "it was carried away with the gear of the mast. He must have swum to it."

"Perhaps his leg floated him up to the beach," chimed in Fisher; "he's got a signal-flag on it now, anyway. Did ever a man see such shooting, though? Why, he doesn't get within fifty yards of them."

"But they'll be within fifty yards of him in a minute, I'm thinking," cried Messenger; "and I'll tell you wnat—this is about the worst business that could nave happened to us. Don't you see that, once these shore-folk know we're lying by, they'll be on top of us with a cargo of redcoats? What then, Burke?"

"Aye, what then?—ez you ask," said Burke, with a repetition of the query. "That nigger's due for a clout on the top in five minutes if we don't step down. But, ye see, there's the boat placed right under our noses. You're not going to pass that by, for sure?".

"I guess not," said Kenner; "not if my word counts one."

"I've thought of that," said Messenger quickly. "We can't leave the boat; that doesn't want discussing. The question is, can we do with another hand, or is the nigger to be left to them?"

"You wouldn't leave the man?" gasped Fisher,

who had frozen at the bold idea. "Why, he's one of us!"

"Maybe," remarked Burke laconically, "but white skins count here afore black; leastwise, where Roger Burke is reckoned with. I'm thinking, though, that if there's to be pistol practice ashore here, the sooner we add to the company the better."

"That's sense," cried Messenger; "we haven't got a dry cartridge amongst us, and he's picked up a rifle; it's worth some risk to get that Winchester. The point is, how are we to get it? If we show up, we shall have shot in us; if we lie low, they'll rap him on the head. But, I tell you what, if we drop behind the bushes down there, and holloa, we may do all we want without showing as much as an arm."

The proposition was agreed to, and they ran along the cliff sharply, descending with the path until they were down upon the beach, but hid by the shelter of the thorn-bushes which bordered upon the sand. Even while they ran the situation of the seaman in the boat had become desperate; for, although he had hit the Spaniard who carried the musket, and the fellow was crawling along the sand in agony, the other two had now come up to the boat, and were laying about them with their cudgels, while the nigger roared like a bull and dealt slashing blows with the butt of his rifle. At this moment the four behind the bushes shouted with all their strength, and at the volley of sound the Spaniards stayed their hands and stood back. But the one-legged man sprang up at the opportunity, and, carrying his rifle in his hand, he hobbled with amazing rapidity of gait towards the cliff, and was in a moment under cover of the shrubbery.

"Come aboard, gemmelen," said he, as he sat down and gasped—"Very warm outside, gemmelen; warm as my country, and a dam sight warmer, sahs —be gor, I've heap plenty shot in me—heap plenty, you take my word, sahs."

He went on thus in his mongrel jargon, but the others did not listen to him, for the Spaniards were standing in consultation by the longboat, apparently undismayed at the volley of the voices, and contemplating, as it seemed, a fresh attack upon the place of sounds. But Messenger, who saw that it was vital to end the delay, took the Winchester rifle which the nigger had carried, and, with fine marksmanship, sent a couple of bullets at them, and hit the taller of the two in the hand at the very moment he was opening the locker in the boat. The fellow uttered a loud cry as the shot struck him, and, a third shot hitting his companion in the arm, the pair made off, reeling like drunken men, and were soon lost to sight behind the projection of the cliff. The third man of their party, who had been wounded at the first bout with the nigger, had already vanished; and, the shore being thus void of men, Burke led the way to the boat, and, caring nothing for Joe's tale of the wondrous method of his escape, they ran the ship into the water, and rowed out rapidly into the bay.

CHAPTER XIII.

THE COVE OF BRANCHES.

IT was now near to mid-day, and the sun beat upon the glassy sea with intolerable strength. While the men rowed from the shore they could see the fiery light glowing upon the caps of the barren hills and lighting even the crannies of the deeper valleys. Over the more open sweeps of grass, which lay amongst the lower pine-woods, herds of swine were roving; and a few sheep hugged the shelter of the spreading woods. But the light was white with a brilliancy which was dazzling, and the driven men, worn with fatigue and doubt and danger, pulled mechanically, and by unspoken consent, to the river's mouth and the shade which it promised to them.

As they came nearer to the neck of the bay, they had the better sight of their haven and of its possibilities. The stream fell from a great height of the mountains to the sea, but there was a deep blue pool where it struck the shore, and about this wooded slopes flanked so steeply that the trees upon their heights hung over the water; and many a cove, roofed with clinging creeper and sheltering bush, offered harbourage from the outer swell. Into one of these, whose mouth was almost hidden by trailing shrubs, the men pulled the boat, to find themselves in that which was almost a cave, though it had a roof of fibrous wood and palm-like leaves, and was the home of a myriad of insects. Here all observation from without was impossible; soft light streamed down through a trellis of green; the air was deliciously cool. For the first time since they had come to Spain the survivors of the *Semiramis* could think, not alone of their immediate circumstances, but of that overwhelming ill which had set them thus upon an inhospitable shore, with the vast treasure for which they had dared such hazards lying, it might be, upon the rocky bed of the reef, or even then swept by the strength of currents into the deeper sea, whence no man should raise it.

In the shadow of the cove Messenger pursued again the idea which had engrossed him since he came ashore.

"Burke," said he, "I was thinking that the tide will be full low about four in the morning. Is that so?"

"It should be," replied Burke, "if tides here ain't as queer as the company."

"In that case, we might pull out at midnight and see what luck we get then. The thing is,— if we should have any luck, what are we to do with the stuff, and how are we to hold it? To me it seems plain enough; we must get a ship—buy one at the nearest port, which you call Ferrol, I believe—and lie low here with the freight until the man that goes for the ship picks us up. It's most cursedly unfortunate that we had a brush with those fellows; but that we must forget. I don't suppose they'll follow us across the bay here, and this seems to me the place to lie in, while we search every yard of the reef we can reach, working always by the dark. There is no earthly reason—providing our suppositions are right—why we should not do well of the venture yet. You won't forget that there are less to share——"

"I was remembering that all along," said Kenner. "There's three in it now, and if half of the load remains we're rich men. For my part, I've a notion, though, that you might as well seek out yonder for greenbacks as for kegs—why, look at the current! Who's seen the like to that?"

"There's current enough," interrupted Burke, as he drew the boat further up the cove and hitched the painter to a root which sprang from the bank, "but that don't concern us. Any child ken see ez the aft cabin is riz up like a load in a cradle. Whether the money lies there or is swep' away you'll learn by looking, and not by talking; and you won't look till the dark falls."

"Meanwhile," hazarded Fisher, who lay his length in the bow of the boat and listened—"Meanwhile, we shall have to forage again; my clock strikes lunch."

J

"Put me down for that," said Kenner; "lunch and another bottle of Spanish vinegar, if it's on tap!—eh, Joe, what are you going to cook for lunch?"

The half-caste had curled himself up astern during the row across the bay, but now he woke up at the mention of cookery, and said—

"Be gor, you cook odd man out, sahs! You cook yourselves by-and-the-by."

"Has anyone thought of searching the locker?" asked Messenger of a sudden. "I suppose you found the rifle there, Joe?"

"Jess, so, sah," said Joe; "I take the liberty to kick him open, and drink your rum, sahs—very good rum; nice long bottle, gemmelen——"

"And a nice long throat!" said Messenger, as he held up a flask of spirit which had lain in the locker of the boat together with a large provision of biscuits, tinned meats, and ammunition both for a pair of Winchester rifles and for Colt's army revolvers. All the boats of the *Semiramis* had been charged thus against peril of the sea; but never did provision come in more handily. There was food enough in this water-tight garner against a week of concealment; and the spirit in particular helped Kenner against his ailments and to strength. Indeed, the meal under the shade of the green haven was near to a merry one, and was flavoured with that salt of excitement and expectancy which in some measure moved them all.

About four of the clock, when the power of the sun had fallen away, and the men had slept heavily upon the hard boards of the boat, they awoke in better hope than they had known since they came to the shore. There was now more suppleness of limb and mind, a greater readiness for activity among them; and they listened to Messenger, who had naturally assumed a dictatorship, with willing ears.

"It's time, now," said he, "that we had a look round us shorewards as well as to sea. I am proposing that Fisher and I make our way to the heights here and prospect, while you three have watch of the boat. A gunshot on either side means that help is wanted; but any man who shows himself when he can lie low deserves what he gets. What I want to find out is if there's a village within two miles of here; and, if so, whether it's a place where we're likely to get aid or the other thing."

They all agreed to this readily, and Fisher having taken a dozen cartridges from the waterproof box in the locker, he left with Messenger on the outpost work. To quit the cave of branches was no easy task —unless they had pulled into the cove, which they did not wish to do; but they contrived to force a path through the trellis of green where it met the bank, and then by climbing nimbly they came up to a verdurous wood which ran by the shore, and into this they plunged.

The wood was dark in the shade of great chestnut-trees, and alive with the hum of myriads of gnats and flies and with the note of birds. It was a strange contrast to the barren hills beyond; but thus is all Galicia, the province of tropical valley and sterile upland, of fine pasturage and iron mountain. The two men, following the shelter of the thicket for some half a mile, could see in the more open glades the herding swine and cattle, with here and there a shepherd lying his length upon the sward; but, beyond the one castle-like building which now presented a fine face, they had no sight either of village or of habitation.

At a distance it might be of a mile from the cove, Messenger, who was going before Fisher, came upon a bridle-path, there being a second branching from this, and leading downwards to the valley. He stopped at the divergent ways, and, speaking in a low tone, he said—

"You take the lower road; but do not show yourself in the open unless you see an object. If you want me, fire once; but you won't do that unless you're in any danger, and that isn't likely unless you run against the men we saw this morning. I trust to you."

Fisher nodded his head for agreement, put his hand upon his pistol to see that it was ready, and went swiftly down the ravine towards the more open woodland. If the truth be written, he had been overcome by no mind for the business since the beginning of it upon the yacht; and the subsequent days did not turn him to affection for it, but left him in doubt if there were one honest man among the company. The business of the money he did not in any way understand; but his faith in Messenger was no longer unquestioning; and, although he had no word to warrant him, he yet knew that a gulf had opened between his one friend and himself, and that nothing coming after could ever bridge it over again. Yet, for the moment, the common necessities of the company compelled him to participate in its actions. He had no manner of proof against the men he judged, no support for his conjecture; he could but theorise, and his theory, being honest, drove him to close action with the survivors of the yacht.

As he thought of these things, descending into the woody valley which lay on the hither side of the mountains, he came, after a sharp walk, into a sylvan glen of the thicket, a shady bower of moss and fern and grass, with a burn splashing in the middle of it and a fringe of low trees set prettily upon its banks. The place was one for concealment, and gave no promise of habitation; but when he thought himself most surely alone, a dog, a Dane of prodigious size, ran up to him inquiringly and forbade advance or even retrogression. No sooner, however, had he drawn back a pace into the wood than the mistress of the dog, a vivacious girl in a cotton frock and an English-looking straw hat, was at the collar of the hound, patting him with a gentle caress and drawing him away to the tree-trunk whereon she had been sitting. Fisher, looking at her across the glade, bethought him that he knew her face; a moment's reflection assured him that he had seen her often before. She was the Spanish girl he had watched curiously at Monaco, the daughter of the woman who had inspired Kenner to such gloomy thoughts and Messenger to such light humour.

This discovery set the lad much at his ease. Messenger, he remembered, had told him to conceal himself from all those who were about the coast, but here at least was a civilised being; Spanish, perhaps, yet none the less to be welcomed in that dismal haven. He had last seen the girl in the whirl of life at Monaco; it must be confessed that he had watched her often interestedly—yet here was she in this wild haven, and surely her presence promised help for the party. Thus he determined to speak to her, believing that the Prince would approve the act; and he advanced from the thicket readily, thinking as he did so what a sorry figure he must cut with his washed-out clothes, his dank hair, and his collarless shirt; and, as the girl stood looking at him amazedly, he said in very ill French, since he had no Spanish—

"I hope I don't frighten you, but I am one of the survivors of a yacht that's been wrecked off here, and I'm looking for the nearest village or something civilised. I thought perhaps you might help me."

The girl heard him with luminous black eyes very

wide open. When she answered, it was in English, as good as his own, though just touched with an accent that gave to it a potent charm.

"I can speak your language," said she, "better than I can speak French. I was educated at Isleworth, near London. I remember you at Monaco; you were with the dark Englishman there. My mother has been away in Italy, but the big house over there is ours, and we expect her to return to-day."

"We seem to be in luck," cried Fisher. "Our yacht went ashore on the bar of the bay, and, so far as we know, there are only five of us left alive. We've had a hard time, and the three men we met on the shore were so glad to see us that they began to shoot when we landed. I was looking for some shelter when I met you, and perhaps some of your people can put us in the way of getting it."

The girl regarded him timorously, stroking the great hound, but hesitating to speak. When she answered, it was with restrained voice, and shyly.

"I am afraid," said she, "that you will find little hospitality in the village of Espasante or anywhere here. There is a coast-guard station at Carnero, and the watchman would be the safest man to go to; or you might ask in the village for the priest, who is named Semello. Our own house is shut up; and even to-day a stranger is not quite safe alone in this wild place. Have you a boat with you?"

"Yes," said Fisher, "the yacht's longboat was washed up sound upon the sand, and if it hadn't been for the biscuit in it we should have wanted a dinner to-day. I was thinking, though, that there would be some house near where we could get food and rest for the day."

"That is because you don't know the coast," said she earnestly; "it's a dreadful place, though I who say it have lived here half my life. If you would listen to me, you would not stay another day here—not another hour—when you can get away."

The girl seemed to speak so earnestly that Fisher, with her words in his ears, bethought him that there was something, at any rate, for Messenger to know, and to know without loss of time. The recollection made him a little abrupt in thanking her who had advised him, and, with a curt word, he turned upon his heel and re-entered the wood. But he had not gone many steps before he heard the Spanish girl's voice, and when he looked round she was running after him with a light pannier of straw in her hands. This she offered to him without a word, though she spoke pity with her great eyes, and her cheeks flushed with the effort she had made. Then she ran off again as she had come; and presently he found the basket to be full of fruit, and to hold a bottle of wine with some fine oatmeal biscuits. His first impulse of the gift was to sit upon the sward and slake his thirst with the luscious grapes; yet he remembered the others and their need, and went straight on towards the shore.

Scarce, however, was he in the dark place of the wood before he heard a crackling of the bushes ahead of him, and, as he stood a moment, a great Spaniard appeared upon the path and held up a cudgel as a signal for him to stop.

CHAPTER XIV.

TO THE CREEK AGAIN.

His first thought, as he saw this man, was one which sprang from early prejudices. He was not altogether wanting the conviction that a Briton is more than the equal of three Frenchmen and a "Portugee," as the old rhyme goes; and the fellow who stood in his path, though a man of great stature, did not alarm him overmuch. Yet he remembered Messenger's injunction, that he should not bring a brawl about him if it were to be avoided; and, with this in his mind, he stood looking at the Spaniard for a moment, and then jumped lightly from the path to the thickness of the undergrowth at the side of it.

Here was an abundance of long grass and shrubs, but principally of sharp-cutting thorns; the ground being soft and boggy, and the weed clinging and tenacious. It seemed to him that a few paces in a marshy slough like this would put all danger behind him; but as he went on forcing his way through the thickness of the bramble there came the whip-like sound of shot about his ears; and he looked back to see the heads of two other men showing between the trees upon his left hand, and he knew that the adventure had become serious.

A second loud report now echoed in the woods and a great eagle-hawk, that he could see stooping down from the infinitely blue sky, stopped in his descent and winged away to the distant hills. This time two of the shots stung him upon the left arm, but he had no other hurt; and he fell upon his hands and knees, leaving the precious basket behind him, and wormed his way with wondrous quickness, though his flesh was cut and his clothes torn to ribbons by the briar through which he went. He could now hear the pursuers tumbling through the bracken behind him, and their fierce shouts, answered again from two or three points in the wood, told him that they set some price upon his capture—indeed, that they meant the worst to him; and, while he was prompted to use his revolver, he hesitated because of Messenger's words and of his own hope of safety.

The way had now become more open, and there was grass in lieu of marsh; but the vociferations of the shoremen were louder; and it seemed to him that they had all come together. They did not shoot any more, however; and when he came to the clearing it was plain to him that he must either up and run for it, taking the risk of the shot, or remain to be knocked on the head for a certainty in the semi-darkness of the glade. He had but the vaguest notion whither the journey would carry him; but he judged that it must be in the way of coming at the creek again; and even as he started to run he remembered the importance of keeping hid the knowledge of the cove and of the men it sheltered. With this thought, he rose up from the ground, and, hunching up his shoulders, he fled like a deer that is hunted, hearing the savage cries redouble as he showed himself, but no gun shot, which surprised him. Anon, he found himself panting up a steep hillside where firs grew thick, but not so as to hamper him; and, as the Spaniards roared the louder and then fell to silence in the ardour of pursuit, he longed for a sight of the sea with a longing he had never known before.

Now, the place where all this happened was a mile or more from the lagoon in which the longboat had been made fast; and Fisher, who thought that he was running towards the neck of the bay, was, in truth moving in a line parallel to it. His path, after it had carried him through the woods (the Spaniards being close upon his heels in the going), brought him at length to the ravine down which the river passed to the sea; and when, wanting his breath to the point of pain, he came out of the woodland, he found himself on the edge of a cañon, at the bottom of which the mountain stream ran swiftly. His position at this time was one of great hazard. His flight had been for the chief part upward, over heavy ground. One of the ragged shoremen following him was not then a hundred yards away; there was before him a precipice with a sheer drop of a hundred feet or more; and he knew that other Spaniards were coming up through the wood, and he expected momentarily to see them.

Driven by the need of the situation, he did then what he had before thought of doing, and fired one shot from his revolver. It was answered by a single shot from another pistol, but upon the other side of the ravine. A moment after, Messenger appeared upon the rocky path which ran along the opposing precipice, and, observing the hazard at a glance, he shouted with echoing strength of voice—

"To the left, man! There's a bridge a hundred yards below you."

Fisher needed no other word than this. Although the bridle-track on which he stood presently inclined so steeply that it fell sheer against the face of an iron cliff, he began to run steadily, with one of his pursuers upon his very heels. A moment after, another appeared on the summit of the rock which shot up on the right hand of his path, and took a heavy stone in his hand, waiting for the runner to pass beneath to hurl it down. Thus the situation stood, that upon one side of the ravine there ran Messenger, and upon the other Fisher, who had a Spaniard at his heels, a second upon the cliff under which he was to pass, and more after him in the shelter of the higher woods. Some of the latter now showed themselves, but upon the upland, debouching from the woods, to cut off the runner before he could reach the bridge of logs which lay a furlong away down the cañon. Had these men possessed muskets, the race would scarce have been run; but, beyond the one fellow who had shot at Fisher in the woods, there was none with better equipment than a cudgel, or a great stone snatched from the path, and they could but run, in the hope of coming up with him at the bridge or striking him down as he trod the ribbon-like track upon the hillside.

Half-way down the path, a shout from Messenger compelled him to stop abruptly. He looked to the height above him, and saw that he had come to a place where one of the Spaniards stood poising a great stone and waiting for his coming. The man was in the very act of hurling the boulder when Messenger fired at him, and the fellow, being hit in the hand, let the rock go crashing down with a reverberating note to the depths of the chasm. At the same moment, a warning cry awakened the lad to the danger behind him, and he turned on his heel sharply to find the man who had pursued him already within arm's length. The fellow had even raised his cudgel for the blow; but, being held quickly, he dropped backward upon the path with the lad holding to his throat.

There never was, it may be, a more hazardous place upon which two men might struggle than this. The track was not three feet wide; the rock rose up sheer on the one side of it; there was the chasm upon the other. Fisher himself had been dragged down upon the burly Spaniard in the fall; and the man had now gripped him about the waist and was making herculean efforts to hurl him over the precipice. He, in turn, had his knee in the fellow's ribs and his hands about his throat; but the man, even in the throes of semi-suffocation drew a sheath-knife from his belt, and made Fisher let go at the throat and clutch the arm which threatened him. But the lad's muscles strained and stood out as he twisted the fellow's hand downwards, and presently he so mastered him that the point of the blade stood turned towards the Spaniard's chest.

In this convulsive and silent fight for sheer footing and for life, the two men were watched by the other Spaniards and by Messenger, none of them moving or crying out; but, when some minutes had gone, the latter called with all his strength to Fisher that he should free himself, for the others were now running swiftly down the path to the help of their man. At this cry the lad raised himself backward by one surpassing effort, and then dropped with his weight again upon the Spaniard, driving the knife deep into his chest, so that the man gave one long groan and then lay still. But Fisher, fearing nothing now but the coming of the others, fled down the path with the shouts of the shoremen in his ears, and was at the hither side of the bridge while the Spaniards yet raved about the body.

Being safely come over the chasm, the two Englishmen now hurried through the woods to the shore, finding as they went that pursuit was not continued. At the foot of the mountain path, when they had crossed a stretch of marsh, they came upon the creek at the opposite side to that by which their boat lay; and, the Spaniards being not in sight, they whistled twice, and the craft put out for them. But no sooner had they made her fast in the cove again, when there was sound of voices in the wood above them, and a boat, which appeared to be that of the coast-guard, appeared in the bay.

CHAPTER XV.

KENNER AGREES.

It was far on in the afternoon, there being a greater red light upon the hills and a deeper purple in the higher ravines. The tide being almost run out of the bay, the strange boat which approached the river kept to the centre of the stream, the men in her having, as those observing her thought, come to shore to learn what was the business of the firing in the upland. A greater misfortune could not, it seemed, have come upon the party; for, on the one hand, there were the Spaniards, wild hillmen of Galicia, who would scarce let the hunt for the strangers lie; and, on the other, the representatives of Spanish authority, to fall into whose hands meant certain extradition to England for the whole of them.

This being so, at the very first sight of the coastguard, Messenger put up his hand for complete silence, having first dragged down the branches over the boat, and whispered to the others to hold her steady. And the whole of them waited with scarce a breath, when the wash of oars sent water rippling into the creek, and eight men in rough uniform, but all armed heavily, rowed across the cove and made fast to the opposite bank.

It is no figure of speech to say that the five hid away under the bushes scarce moved a hand during this manœuvre. They were in some part relieved to find that the men made no attempt to search the banks of the cove (nor, indeed, did the Spanish guard suspect the presence of a boat upon the shore); but their uneasiness was greater when seven of the eight ran up to the hills and were heard whistling one to the other in the high places. What they did there, or whether the shoremen fled at their coming, in some part fearing that their share in the adventure should be discovered, the others never knew; for by-and-by they came again as they had gone, and, without as much as a look at the bushes, they rowed straight out towards the headland, and, indeed, towards the rocks where the end of the *Semiramis* had been.

At the sight of this course, Kenner could no longer keep silence—

"Prince," said he, with a ghastly face, "they're rowing straight for the reef—did ye see that?"

"I did," said Messenger, curtly. "Do you suggest that we should row after them?"

"But," cried Kenner, "they'll find the money——"

"Possibly," said Messenger. "It will be found by the first man that touches the point—if they're going there, they'll bring it back with them."

"He's right," cried Burke, though he ground his

teeth; "and they're laying dead on the tack. Look at 'em now!"

The boat, as he said, was holding on the tack, the course being set, as it seemed, straight out to sea. Once or twice there broke from the American snarling curses and muttered oaths, but Messenger sat very still, with deeper lines in his face, and his hands moved restlessly, as the hands of a nervous man will. Thus it was for one terrible quarter of an hour, when the distant boat went up the bay; but at the last a shout, which was not to be held back, burst from the five, and Kenner sobbed like a woman. The coastguard had pulled round the headland, and the bay was empty.

"That," said Messenger, when the critical moment was obviously past, "was the worst ten minutes of my life;" and he wiped from his forehead the sweat which streamed upon it. But Kenner was already helping himself to the rum, and the others drank, while Fisher began to tell them what had passed on shore, and to try and mend his rags. When he spoke of his meeting with the Spanish girl, Kenner looked up quickly, but checked the words upon his lips, and relapsed into moody silence, sitting through the whole narration as one thinking. Had Messenger noticed him, he would have remembered his words at Monaco, when he said that he would meet the Spanish woman again; but the necessities of the moment outweighed any recollections, and Kenner maintained his silence until Fisher concluded. At the end of his tale, and when they had made a pretty bandage of one of his hands, which was sorely injured, Burke cut in with his advice—

"Look now," said he; "it's mighty poor fortune, but, ez far ez I ken see, when we put our feet in that hog-sty this morning we went for to stir up blazes. You may bet that the man in the boots told his chaps, and they told other chaps, and it's round the town by this time, if ez there is a town. What you're going to do, heaven knows, Prince. I've rid roads in my time; but I was never so near to the floor—never, as I'm living——"

"Wall," said Kenner, who at this forced himself to speak, "I've thought your way since morning; if you'd be asking for my word, I'd say let the stuff lie, and be d——d to it. There's money ashore if you live to get it; but what's your chance when it's more than your neck's worth to show in a town, and you've no craft to work in but a cockleshell, which won't carry you ten mile in a sea, let alone against the kind of sea you've got to face to make Ferrol?"

"All that's true enough," replied Messenger, who had listened to them very patiently; "but it's argument that's as narrow as the bridge of your nose. In the first place, how do you think we've any chance of walking through Spain without a shilling in our pockets, when, by this time, we must be papered on every shore in Europe? In the second, how do you propose to get out of Spain and reach the other side until you've touched some of the freight that you're now talking about as though it was to be had at sixpence a pound? Why not say at once that none of you have yet realised what you were playing for? Where I am concerned, I shall stay here as long as I can walk; but any of you that chooses had better go now."

"Where you stop, I shall stop," said Kenner; "you know me well enough for that. Not that I don't think you're right; you're right all along. We've sat on the stuff and fed on it, yet there's not a man among us but yourself who knows what it would look like if rolled out on this shore in sovereigns. And that's nat'ral, I guess. But as for being with you, I'm with you to the end."

"You may pass that round," said Burke, as the man shook hands—a practice beloved of every American—and then he continued with satisfaction, "I reckon, Prince, ez your talk is like oil to a lamp—it lights all of us. Once the load is ashore here, and we've got our arms in it, there's a dozen roads to take. What I'm looking for now is dark—the sooner the better."

"And an hour's sleep," said Messenger; "there's nothing like a doze to clear the mind, and we don't want any thick heads for the work we've got before us. The nigger there will watch, for he's slept all day."

"Be gor, sah," said the nigger; "you think I sleep, you labour under a lie, sah; watch better with eyes shut, sah—presarve the sight, by golly."

"I'm thinking if you sleep this watch that there'll be darned little of you to preserve, anyway," said Burke; and with that they all turned in, and not a man of them moved until dark was down upon the sea, and from the distant cape the light shone flickering and feeble, as do so many of the headland lanterns on this desolate coast. At that hour, Messenger, huddled up amidships, shook himself like a dog; and when he had sat up, he awakened the others; but to the nigger he gave a fierce kick, for the man was heavy with sleep, and lay hunched up in the bows. All being thus aroused, they pushed out the boat silently from the cove; and, scarce daring to use their oars, crept to the bay in the shelter of the dark, and then rowed with that fierce excitement and brooding expectancy which were so entirely the outcome of the situation.

Was the gold still lying in the poop of the ship, or had the hull broken up so completely that the kegs had gone swirling away in the current to be lost in the deep of the sea beyond the headlands? Would they ever look upon that power of treasure again, or was it engulfed with the unnumbered dead, and the ships of the ages, and the wealth of cities and of nations which the Atlantic has fed upon in her victories? Had any from the shore anticipated them? If they recovered the gold, could they drag it through Spain with them? These were but a tithe of the questions they asked themselves as they drove the boat over the shallows of the bay, and onward, until the greater waves touched her, and she began to rise upon the swell of the bar. Then all eyes were turned to the reef; and when the first of the crags of rock seemed to take shape from the sea, when it rose before them as a dark pinnacle, Burke uttered a low cry of exultation, for the poop stood clear above the water, and in the stillness there was no wave so great that it broke upon it.

A few strokes now carried them to the cradle of rock in which the last of the *Semiramis* lay. Though this presented a sheer face to the land, it fell away on the far side of the bar; and the men, bringing the boat under shelter of the crag, waited until the sea should fall, for it was yet but an hour after high water.

When at last the ebb set in more rapidly, Burke sprang from the bows to the plateau with nimble step; and, being come up on the poop, he presently disappeared into the cabin. But the others waited with a great silence upon them, robbed of words by the moment of his mission; yet possessing full knowledge of the meaning both of good tidings and of bad.

CHAPTER XVI.

GOLD FROM THE SEA.

THE interval of waiting seemed interminable. The four in the boat, holding to the jutting pinnacle of rock with difficulty, could hear the lapping of the water in the wreck and the rush of the tide as it swept through the gullies of the reef. But they feared to speak, scarce dared to breathe fully, were oblivious of the hazard of their own position, a position to be held only in unusual stillness of the sea.

Yet Burke did not come, and gradually there crept upon them the chill of a great fear—the fear that the gold was swept out to the depths of the bay, and that their all-venturing emprise had brought them nothing but beggary and peril. Even Fisher, upon whose mind suspicion of half the truth had long weighed, forgot in that weird and passionate excitement, which the gain or loss of bullion ever excites, the impulses which had troubled him. The spell of expectation was too strong, the import of the moment too engrossing.

Now, Burke was in the wrecked cabin no more than five minutes, but the anxiety of the men waiting had led them to magnify the moments ridiculously; and when he came on deck again Kenner, who stood in the prow of the longboat, could no longer restrain himself.

"Burke!" he shouted, "for God's sake speak!— have ye found anything?"

To this shout of a question Burke gave no answer, but he beckoned them with his hand to come aboard; whereupon Messenger and Kenner, leaving the others to hold the boat against the rush of the tide, sprang up to the deck, and stood with him. The American was quivering with fear, but the Prince showed no emotion, though he said as he came to the broken booby-hatch—

"I'm supposing that it's worth our while to go below;" and with that he swung himself down the rope that Burke had hitched aft, and entered the saloon. But Kenner continued to stand upon the slippery deck, while the nerves of his face twitched, and he could not keep his hands still. A moment later, Messenger clambered up as he descended; burst into a hearty fit of sniggering laughter—the nervous result of the unspeakable strain.

"Good heaven!" said Kenner as he saw him, "can none of ye speak? Is the money there, or is it not? By gosh, my heart's going right round like a windmill! Man, it's more than I can bear!"

The Prince ceased to laugh, observing the other's strong distress, and gave him his hand.

"Kenner," said he, "come and look for yourself

So far as I can see, every shilling of the bullion is just where I left it."

"What!" cried Kenner; and with that he rolled over upon the deck in a faint, so that if Burke had not held him he would have gone down into the sea. He was then a man worn with the want of food and with exposure; and, although his dizziness passed away as he fell, they put him back into the boat, making that fast to the taffrail, and called the nigger aboard the yacht to help them. It was not a moment for words, and no man spoke; but the three went at once to the saloon and began their labour while night shielded them.

To the complete understanding of this remarkable preservation of the bullion, the position of the yacht upon the reef is the key. She had run upon a small group of rocky islets standing, as the Admiralty chart shows, more than a mile from the tongue of land near Cape Celstigos. Her prow being caught in the claw-like grip of scissor-like projections of rock, the stern had swung round until it had rested upon a cup-shaped ridge, which had raised it above the immediate wear of the sea; and left it exposed completely at the ebb, and scarce covered at the top of the tide. This being the position of the ship as she struck, she had subsequently broken in two; but the stern of her, with its bulkhead intact, had sunk into the cup, and suffered little hurt beyond the ripping of the bottom and the flood of the water. Naturally, the heavy kegs of gold had stood unharmed; and, as the grey light of the summer's night came down through the broken skylight, those who looked saw the whole of the bullion stacked as they had left it; though one keg had burst, and ingots of gold shone with wondrous lustre amongst the wreckage upon the floor.

If this was the case with the gold, elsewhere in the fetid saloon the destruction was complete. The whole place reeked of damp and foulness; the fine upholstery was slime-hid and dripping; there was water gushing upon the floors. It was pitiable to see gaudy travelling-bags with oozy mud upon them, and the little library of books washed to pulp; but for that the men had no eyes. They had already begun to work, and the damp of perspiration rolled off them as they hauled the kegs on deck, and passed them quickly to the rolling boat below. Nor did they cease or speak to one another until the longboat was drawing dangerously low in the water; and it was evident that repeated journeys would be necessary to save from the sea the rich freight it held for them. Then, in their common perplexity, they stayed their hands and faced the question.

"I tell you my opinion right here," cried Burke, who was the first to perceive the trouble. "If you put another keg on that boat, she'll go under—look at her now!"

"I've just thought it," said Messenger; "and there's ourselves to go aboard yet. When do you look for day?"

"I'm looking for it now," said Kenner; "you can't gainsay that there's light from the sun yonder."

He pointed to the higher headlands to the east of them, now beginning to shape in a cold steely light that passed slowly from hill to hill, and showed mist rising from the valleys. Dawn had come upon them as they worked; and as day spread upon the sea they began to realise that their haphazard method had not befriended them.

"It seems to me," said Messenger, as he sat upon the hatch and looked all around him despairingly, "that we haven't got the sense of a fly amongst us! This cargo won't be stored under three journeys, and the first is not to be made now. We should have run ashore with the dark."

"I guess that's so," cried Burke, squirting the juice of his tobacco, which he had dried, over the taffrail; "there's no moving from here until night, and we're up in luck if there's none of 'em sight us from the shore afore then. What we've got to do now is to make her snug, and there ain't time to lose. If the sea rises, you'll be swimming agen."

In truth, their loitering had placed them in no pleasant situation. The sea was then still enough, a misty white fog rolling up from it with the sun; and it beat placidly with a long swell upon the outer reef, while a full sweet breeze came off the land, but with no strength. Their difficulty was to get a suitable anchorage with such a heavily-laden craft, but they brought the boat, after some hazardous manœuvring, to the shoreward side of the crags, and there lay right under the rock-cradle upon which the poop of the yacht rested. It was agreed that one man should squat by the higher rock through the tide to watch the coming of boats; and Fisher, being the more nimble, went first to this duty, while the others got at the biscuit and the rum for lack of any other breakfast.

For the space of an hour the situation in which the men found themselves was not unpleasant. There was a gentle warmth upon the sea and a soothing lap of the tide which conduced to rest. Fisher, who had diversified his watch by searching in the higher lockers of the saloon, had found there two boxes of cigars comparatively free of damp, and several bottles of liquor, with some cases of preserved fruits, which he passed down to the boat, while he himself made no poor meal, though he would willingly have bartered the whole of the yellow Chartreuse for a cup of sound coffee. The better fare, however, conduced to general content, and when Burke had asked to be roused on the approach of any ships whatsoever, the four in the boat slept soundly, as men wasted with excitement and with fear.

During the early hours of the morning Fisher, who had perched himself upon a cranny high up in the reef, watched the rolling tide and the empty face of the bay. Flowing slowly, yet with fiercer swish of water in the gullies, the sea rose about the needles of black rock, beginning to pour again upon the bullion, and to roll into the reeking saloon. The sun now shot a brilliant spread of dazzling light upon the distant woods and hills, and showed the hulls of fishing boats away to the westward, where they came from Santa Marta, though he who saw them was in ignorance of this. Once, perhaps in the third hour of the morning watch, a small passenger steamer passed within a couple of miles of the reef; but Fisher crouched low upon his ledge as she went, and she made no sign that she had observed anything. Then for a full hour more nothing but the dark shapes of far-distant luggers occupied the sea; and so it stood until the turn of the others had almost come. At this time, however, the lad, suddenly standing right upon the pinnacle to get a better sweep of the sea, observed many miles distant, but unmistakable, the shape of a larger ship than any he had yet seen, and, wanting trust in himself to be sure of her description, he at once called to Burke.

"What is it?" said the latter, awaking drowsily at his call. "By thunder! I thought I'd a dozen Spaniards atop of me. Is it ez you see anything?"

"There's a ship steering in from N. by W.," said Fisher. "I think you'd better look at her."

The boat had now risen above the main ledge of rock, and Burke clambered up there with difficulty. When he had looked a moment at the distant ship, he gave a low whistle, and called up Messenger.

"What do you make of that?" he asked. "By the

look of her she's British, and coming near in the bay if she can."

Messenger looked long and anxiously before he answered.

"I believe you're right," said he at last; "she's the cut of the *Eclipse*, and she certainly seems to be coming in here. It's a tight place to face, but the first thing to do is to lie low; they could sight us through a glass now, and we must just hang on by our eyebrows. Down you go, Burke, while I think it out."

They both went down at his words, sitting hunched around the crag with their legs in the water; but first they shouted to Kenner in the boat to bring her as close under the rock as might be possible, and they sent Fisher, to whom the new excitement was as meat and drink, back to the boat to help with the oars.

"Now," said Messenger, "the thing begins to shape itself. If they're coming here because news of our being ashore has got abroad, they'll steer straight for the reef, and we'll simply have to walk aboard them. On the other hand, they may be cruising round. Burke, is it to be stay or go?"

"Ez for me," says Burke, "I don't see where she's got tidings of us—leastwise, by this time. I should stay. If you go ashore now, what does it mean? Why, it means ez you'll have all the folk from five mile round come to look at you. At the worst, you can run it agen the ship's boat if she puts one out."

"Of course we can," cried Messenger. "And if we get a mile start, we can take the odds on shore; but we're going to have a bad ten minutes."

"But it's stay, I reckon," said Burke; "and a wash throw'd in with it. I'm up to my hips in salt!"

He spoke with no exaggeration; and for the next hour the pair of them, with their legs down into the sea, sat motionless while a cruiser of the *Melampus* type—but whose name they could not read—steamed slowly across the bay. It was infinitely fortunate for them that the tide was nearly at its height when the ship passed by the reef, for the high water almost hid the wreck of the yacht, and the other stood away at least three miles from the shore; yet was every cable's length she made an agony to them.

When they had watched thus for half-an-hour, questioning each other as anxious men will, the cruiser ceased to steam opposite to the headland, and they observed that she was signalling; but now she moved again, and although the fear-stricken men scarce dared to speak to each other of hope, she ultimately steamed out of the bay, and was lost upon the eastern horizon.

CHAPTER XVII.

THE FIGHT IN THE CABIN.

So overwhelmingly fierce was the sun at twelve o'clock, that the crew of the longboat suffered intolerably. The early breeze of morning fell away altogether at eight bells, and a torrid, sweltering light poured down pitilessly upon the rock. In this, however, the men had fortune with them, that no boats from the shore came near the reef; and they lay unmolested, though suffering much, until the first welcome failing of the light. Then, with no more delay, they began to row with powerful strokes towards the further land, and to realise for the first time the import of the cargo they carried.

When they had come well into the bay, and lay upon their oars to consider upon a place of landing, the difficulties of the previous day readily recurred to them. It was clear that the Spaniards with whom they had been brought to a brawl would continue to look for them at the pool of the stream; and such a haven was no longer to be thought of. Yet a rapid survey of the bay had shown to them the outline of

L

a village on its eastern side, and this they could not approach, nor the headland to the westward, which had the watch-tower upon its summit. And in this perplexity they remained for a long spell, while the boat drifted in the loom of the land.

"It just comes to this," said Messenger, when they had argued the matter for the tenth time, "we must find a place we can hold while one of us gets to Ferroll and brings a ship. For that purpose we shall want something a little stronger than bushes above us; and we don't look to camp in this ship, it may be for a week, it may be for two. My own inclination sends me round the eastward headland, there to learn what's beyond the village; and, if there's no ground likely, it won't kill us to pull back again."

"If my inclination led me, I should shift straight for a square meal and a long drink at the nearest bar," responded Kenner, dolefully; but, finding that he had no sympathy from the others, who put the boat at once upon the course Messenger had indicated, he turned to the nigger and addressed him with sorrow; to which the man responded with a great show of teeth and an ambiguous "By golly!" He meant to convey the intimation that he was hungry; but so, indeed, were all of them, though there could be no leisure for food, neither then nor for many hours. And they rowed in a determined silence right round the eastern headland, standing in the dark a couple of miles away from the village, and coming at length to a second bay, which was not so deep as the other; but had cliffs of repelling steepness and seemingly impregnable face.

Here they coasted for a half-mile or more, until at last the cliffs, though of continuing height, were split into close ravines of whitish earth, and showed numberless inlets and tiny creeks—some of them with a stretch of sandy beach, others shoreless fjords. It was the work of an hour or more to explore the first half-dozen of these with any exactitude; but, after many rejections and selections, they put at last into a natural harbour which seemed to be cut by Nature just for their own purpose. Not only did a channel of the sea, some eight feet wide, run into this haven, giving water even at the bottom of the tide, but the passage turned some thirty feet from the shore, and there disclosed a perfect fjord. Cliffs of great altitude, almost shut out the sky; a still basin of water gave to the retreat all the aspect of a lagoon. It was entirely such a harbour as they might have prayed for; and when, they being just come to the head of it, the moon sent radiating beams down through the white cañon and a thousand pinnacles of rock glinted in the yellow light, there was a wild picturesqueness about their haven which surpassed description.

Burke's first exclamation when the boat grounded was one of delight.

"If there's a finer spot for throwing the stuff ashore between here and Lisbon, I'll give you my share," said he; and with that he sprang upon the beach, and the others followed him, stretching themselves as men whose limbs were racked with cramp and confinement. To haul the ship up was not their purpose; but they forced her broadside to the sand, and then, at Messenger's dictation, they began to act.

"Now, boys," said he, and he spoke exultingly, "out with the stuff; there's another journey to be made before dawn, and the night's short enough any way."

In half an hour kegs and cases lay piled upon the sand, and the boat stood high in the water. Then Burke, who had taken a hasty sounding, gave his advice for the disposition of the cargo with a readiness which again emphasised the quick working of a curiously ill-balanced brain.

"Look you," said he, "there's a rock bottom at the turn of the passage, and a pool two feet deep here. You couldn't want better, if it had been made for you. Drop the stuff there, and there it lies till the Day of Judgment for all the sea'll do to it."

At these words, they rolled the freight into the sea-pool, where it sank with a heavy splash; and then, scarce consenting to wait, as Burke insisted, for a cloud which was coming up with a gentle westerly wind to cover the moon, they pushed out heedlessly to sea, and by dawn a second load lay in the calm water of the cove, and the men prepared in the light of the day for their own concealment and for that of their boat.

As the morning light flooded their haven, yet left it dim, for the sky above them where the cañon opened was black with rain clouds, they began to see their environment and its possibilities. On either side of them was a wall of rock, but on the left side the precipice was split into irregular ridges. The first of these, at the height of five feet or less, appeared to form a rude path, leading through the cañon to the hill-land beyond it. It was this ledge which the quick eye of Messenger selected for the camping place, and having hauled himself up to it, he found by walking no more than fifty yards that there was a hollow under the rock where the whole of them could be in shelter and almost absolute concealment.

In such a retreat they camped during that day, feeding upon the biscuits and the fruit, and suffering their insatiable hunger for meat; but early in the night, leaving Kenner in charge of the haven, the other four put out again; and, holding off the land in their hope of escaping all observation, they came, after rowing for a couple of hours, within a quarter of a mile of the reef before they were able to observe it closely.

The moon had not yet risen; and the night was dark with storm-cloud. The westerly wind, which had been increasing since the dawn, blew freshly, and they could see the silver of surf beating up upon the pinnacles and flecking them with foam. This deterred them in no way, but having ceased to row for a spell that they might shape the best course possible to make the inner pool, they were suddenly startled by a low cry from Fisher, who had the tiller, and whose eyes were glued upon the reef.

"Prince," said he, "is that a man moving on the poop there, or can't I see straight!"

"By gosh! it *is* a man!" said Burke, and the nigger, chiming in, cried—

"Two men, sah, and a keg for to lug, by golly!"

If shot had come among them, you could not have surprised them more sharply. For a long spell they sat speechless, laying upon their oars and watching the two fellows who were well occupied hauling one of their kegs into a boat anchored on the shoreward side of the islets; but whose mast stood above the ledge with a triced-up lug-sail flapping to the breeze. So busy were they that no sound of the approaching ship's boat had disturbed them; nor did they see her as she lay with her crew stupefied and wordless. And when they had lowered the keg of bullion they disappeared into the cabin again, unconscious of observation or of danger. But Messenger had already made up his mind, and pulling out his revolver, he said—

"Burke, if a man amongst them goes ashore living, the game's up. Have you got any cartridges in your belt?"

"I've half a dozen, and five in the shooting-iron." replied Burke. "What's the youngster got?"

"He'll stand by the boat," said Messenger quickly,

"and come aboard only when I call him. Are you quite ready?"

"Aye, aye," cried Burke; and upon that they shot the boat with rapid strokes to the inner pool of the reef, and sprang nimbly to the poop.

A lantern was burning in the depth of the cabin, and by its light they saw two men bending over a case of sovereigns which they had broken open, and whose dazzling contents held them spell-bound.

Though the light was dim enough, and burnt flickeringly, the saloon shone with a dazzling radiance which was blinding to the eyes. Before the astonished men there lay a fortune of gold; a cube of sovereigns pressing thick upon each other; a mass of glittering, scintillating metal, which was as a sun to the cabin. To bathe their hands in it, to pour it in cupfuls back to the treasure-box, to listen to the chink of it—this was the occupation of the two Spaniards upon whose vision such a sight had come; and it held them indifferent to sound and suspicion, cast upon them that inexplicable spell which is the potency of treasure. But to the others watching, the spectacle was one which moved every impulse of greed; and stifling words with difficulty, they prepared to leap down the ladder and begin the attack.

"Mark your man," said Messenger, in a whisper, "and shoot straight. They'll have knives, and it's best fought apart. I go first."

He went lightly down the ladder as he spoke, and the Spaniards immediately turning, he shot at the one upon the left hand; but the fellow raised his arm as the trigger fell, and the bullet split the bone of it, and spent itself in the far cushions. The other, with a pitiful cry upon his lips, whipped out his knife and dropped under the wrecked table, where Burke shot at him twice; and each time he groaned, as though the bullet had burnt his body. But the lantern had rolled over at the jar, and, in the utter darkness (for they yet lacked the light of the moon), Messenger closed in upon the fellow who had been wounded, and hugged him in a fierce embrace, so that he bawled with the pain of the arm which was broken; and yet fought to hold off the revolver which was so near to his temple. Such a struggle could scarce have endured for two minutes but for the intervention of the man under the table, who of a sudden slashed with his knife at Messenger's legs, and cut one of them from the knee-cap to the shin. The smart of the wound compelled the Prince to let his man loose, and, flinging him with a great effort upon the floor, he deliberately shot at his body as he lay; but the pain had unnerved him, and at the fourth shot only did the Spaniard quiver and his limbs draw up in the contraction of death.

It was now a horrid scene. One of the Spaniards was dead, as they thought; the other hid behind the cases, craving for mercy and shaking in all his limbs. To shoot at this man was impossible, even had there been light by which to load; but the dark was unbroken, and they knew the hiding-place only

"BURKE SHOT AT HIM TWICE" (*p.* 184).

when they saw gleaming eyes, as the eyes of a brute, shining up from the shadow; or heard the muttered prayer of one to whom death was very near. Others, perchance, would have let the man go, leaving him at the worst a prisoner upon the rock. But the lust of the gold and the terror of pursuit were upon the men; and, having whispered together, they suddenly stepped over the cases, and, as the cowering sailor rose up to receive them, Burke struck at his head with his revolver, and Messenger gripped his arm with all the strength left to him.

For some moments the three rocked in desperate embrace. Burke had missed his blow, and, staggering, had fallen across the chest of the Spaniard, who dug the nails of his left hand into his throat, and promised to throttle him every time he renewed his grip. The very fall of the giant skipper prevented the Prince aiming a blow at the Spaniard's head, and he needed the strength of both his hands to cope with the tremendous arm which held the sheath-knife. Thus for a spell they rolled about on the floor, the one now as fierce as the two, enraged and hopeless in the terrible combat. Indeed, the daring of his struggle was beyond description; and Burke was upon the very point of unconsciousness, when a chance move brought it to an end.

The great American was, as I have said, near to being choked. So strong was his agony that he rolled at last right round under the Spaniard's clutch; and thus turning his body, the sheath of his knife struck Messenger's leg. Burke himself could not speak; but his partner felt the touch of the haft, and, holding to the doomed man's arm with one of his hands only, he drew Burke's blade from the sheath quickly, and, with savage strength, he drove it into the body below him. Yet still the man was not done with, for, as the others rose up, he of a sudden, in the horrid contraction of his muscles, slashed fiercely with the hand that held his knife; and at the stroke he laid open Burke's face from the temple to the chin, sending the huge scoundrel howling from the cabin to the deck, where he lay, with oaths upon his lips, near blinded with his blood. Thither Messenger followed him, white and sick with the shock of reaction, sweat gathering thick upon his forehead, his ragged clothes torn the more, his leg scarred and slashed—yet with his nerve as ready and his purpose as set as at the beginning of it.

"Burke," he cried, when he came to the top of the companion, "where are you?—did you get cut, man?'

"Cut!" yelled Burke, "cut! Look at me; I guess there's coals on my cheek—burn his body! I'm blinded."

Messenger bent down and looked at the upturned and hideous face. He shuddered as he saw it, and, pulling at his soft linen shirt, he tore off a great piece and bound up the wound clumsily, while the other howled childishly with the pain of it.

"That'll hold you till we're ashore," said the

Prince, as he worked with deft fingers; "get into the boat and take a pull at the spirits—you there, Joe bring her in and come aboard."

"Aye, aye," sang out the man, and with the words he brought the nose of the boat up to the rock, and Burke staggered into it, falling prone when he had made the step, and lying like a hulk by the bow-thwart. But the nigger jumped to the rock, and, descending the companion, began to haul up the remaining kegs; and at last, with prodigious labour, they raised the case of sovereigns, though the roughly fastened lid came off again, and sent many coins jingling upon the steps and to the floor.

Of the bullion, all, with the exception of two small kegs, was now either sunk in the white haven or stowed in the longboat; but one keg lay near the body of the dead Spaniard, and his left hand rested upon it. The light in the cabin was at this time somewhat better, and Messenger, taking a last look round, observed the forgotten plunder, and made a step forward to take it; but the upturned visage of the dead man was so repellent, there was such a distortion of feature and of form, that the observer was seized for the first time with uncontrollable terror, and he rushed from the cabin with a cry in his throat. The sharp air, for the west wind was now blowing strongly, nerved him again, but not to dare the saloon. He knew that he would not look upon that face again for ten kegs of the bullion, and he strove to send the nigger in his place. But the man howled out at the suggestion, and fell upon his knees imploringly.

"De Lord help me, sah, I not touch it; I not go there; he look at me, sah!"

"Then get up for a fool," snarled Messenger; and he gave him three sound kicks, which sent him headlong into the longboat.

The wind now blew almost a gale, and the sea was beginning to surge heavily upon the reef. Fisher, who had sat at the tiller of the longboat through the whole affair, and upon whom the fight had come as a revelation, compelling him to see of what kind were the men his friends, still kept the nose of the boat towards the centre of the pool; but Messenger called upon him to take an oar, and he obeyed as a man who hears, but can make no answer. The nigger was at the bow thwart; and, thus manned, they backed out the ship to the rough of the open, and were preparing to row for the shore when a new idea arose.

"Hold her there," cried Messenger. "I'd clean forgotten the keg in their boat. Back astern, stroke, and paddle on, bow."

The Spaniards "ketch" had been made fast in the inner channel, the painter being hitched to a boat-hook driven into a crevice. She now rode uneasily, labouring in the fresher wind. A dog curled up in the cuddy barked loudly as the longboat ran alongside.

"When we've got the keg, and before we let her go," said Messenger on the ships touching,

THE FIGHT IN THE CABIN. 189

"we might see if there's anything to eat aboard. Just climb up, Hal, and look; but don't be long about it."

Fisher went doggedly with the nigger, while the other held with boat-hooks to the shrouds of the smack. The sea was then so fresh that it was no easy matter to reach the ketch's deck, and, once there, the lad needed a seaman's feet to keep his hold. Yet this he scarcely noticed, for his thoughts were about the scene in the other cabin, and the light which it had thrown upon the character of the one man he called a friend. What desperate adventure was he embarked upon? he asked himself again and again. How came it that the companion who had shown through long years the placid face of an emotionless being had become of a sudden a madman or a fiend? The answer took in his mind a hundred shapes, but all of them reflected only his own helplessness, or seemed to tell him to hold his tongue and go through with it. There was no other course; yet he knew that now he stood alone, and fell to wondering about the future both of the others and of himself.

These things, I say, he thought, as he rolled the keg to the lifeboat and searched the ship's cabin, wherein there was a stove burning with the embers of charcoal; but they passed for a moment from his mind when the dog came to him and barked a truce. The truth was that when he beat open the locker of the cabin and took therefrom two great hunks of coarse meat, with a sack of biscuit, some rye-bread. and another sack of potatoes, he knew the adventurer's joy at the prospect of food, and in that matter was at one with the others of the party. Thus it came that he found himself crying out childishly as he hurled the things down to the longboat and Messenger stored them.

"Don't forget the water, if you can lift it," cried the latter, "and throw any spare rope there is; we shall want it yonder."

This was a wise thought, and Fisher quickly rolled the two kegs from the waist of the ship to the side, and, with the nigger's help, got them aboard. Then, having also taken all the ropes they could lay hands upon, they pushed off and let go the ketch's painter, at which she drifted slowly for some moments until the current took her, and she went swirling away, with the dog barking pitifully at the taffrail. She was out of sight in five minutes, and then began that long and laborious row to the distant haven—a row which might never have been accomplished but for the fact that tide and current swept strongly under them, and that the wind, full from the west, eased their labour. Yet they dared not to sail, so strong was the breeze; and, when they had rowed for an hour, the light on the headland beyond their bay was still afar off.

During this journey, Burke lay in a state of semi-insensibility near the bows. Fisher had suggested giving him water, but Messenger intervened, crying to let him lie. He, for his part, cared nought whether the man lived or died; and all his hope was that of getting quickly to the creek where Kenner waited. After that, the future would be easier; but at the moment it was as doubtful as the night above them. With this in his mind, he urged the others to greater effort; but scarce had he spoken when the rowers ceased suddenly to work and a cry broke from all of them.

For with his words a gun boomed out over the sea by the far headland, and a rocket left a fiery trail upon the curtain of the sky.

CHAPTER XVIII.

SEA-WOLVES AT WORK.

THE gun-shot and the flare of the rocket (as I say) stopped the rowers in their work. For a while they sat waiting for a second report, or for some light upon the origin of the first; and they did not move until an answering rocket leaped up from the headland in their bay, and another from the watch-tower upon the promontory at which they had first come ashore. These flights of fiery light drew a second gun-shot from the sea, and at that Messenger made up his mind.

"There's either a ship ashore," said he, "or they've smelt out Kenner in his hole. That's bad for us, anyway, for there'll be coastguards down on the beach, and ships about from somewhere. If I'm not mistaken, there are lights moving in the village yonder already."

"Be gor! plenty lanterns there, sah!" cried the nigger. "What you say 'bout this country, sah?—all cut-throat here by de profession, sah."

"There's no doubt about the lanterns," interposed Fisher; "and I believe I see a couple of small boats rounding the headland. It must be a ship ashore, and they're going to bring off the crew."

At this Messenger smiled.

"If there's any crew brought off to-night," said he, "Galicia isn't what I thought it. It's lucky for us any way. We may get through while those ashore are flying at other game."

The ship, which, as they came to know afterwards, had gone ashore in the shallows of the second bay, now fired more guns; but the wind blew so strongly, sending spray clean over the longboat, even in the calmer water on the hither side of the reef, that they could but just hear them, and they began to row again. They had taken twenty strokes, perhaps when the nigger let go the handle of his oar once more, and, with a "Lord, have mercy!" covered his eyes. The others, looking over the side as he pointed, saw the corpse of a man, turned upon its back, and showing a white face, over which the spray sported as if in victory. So close came the dead man to them that they could perceive the water rushing in and out of his opened mouth; but the eyes, fixed and lustreless, did not move at the touch of the sea, and the hair upon the forehead lay dank and streaming.

A second corpse—that of a woman, with black hair, and the mark of terror still binding the features to distortion—now touched gently against the prow of the longboat, only to be carried more swiftly out upon the broad of the bay to the waste of water and the loneliness of the night. For one moment the derelict body, about which there was a life-belt, hugged the shelter of the gunnel; then it went onward, passing out in the black swirl of the current to the fury of the breakers in the open. But the watching men, speaking no word one to the other, rowed on the faster, as though wishing to shut the sight from their eyes, and the horror of it from their minds.

They had now come well into their own bay, but two luggers passed them as they went, and they lay on their oars breathlessly; but were not seen, so keen were the wolves to reach the carcase of the ship. It was vastly harder work, this rowing in the bay, for the current flowed right round it and against them; and for more than an hour they pulled desperately,

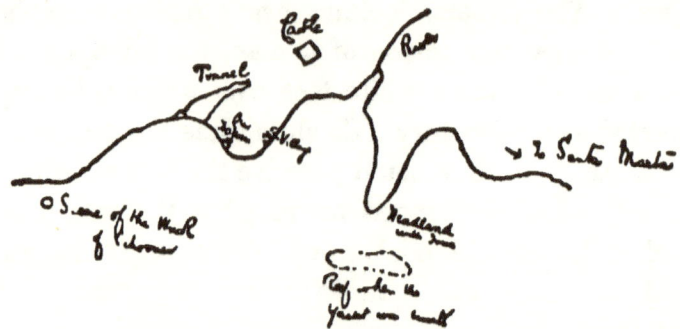

[This rough map, drawn by Hal Fisher, is reproduced to give some idea of Messenger and his party after the bullion was landed. It will be observed that there are consecutive bays on this part of the coast of Galicia, the men having come to shore in the centre bay, and finally taken refuge in the one upon the left hand.—ED. "Sea Wolves."]

still observing lanterns upon the shore, and many lights over against the point by which the trouble was. They were now so near that the sound of voices came to their ears; and the cries as of men fighting, and others encouraging them, were to be heard above the sough of the wind. But the headland of the bay sheltered them from the rougher waves they had known in the open; and a final effort brought them to the cove and to the inner lagoon where Kenner was awaiting them, though exceeding anxious for their coming and the safety of the camp.

"Hello," said he, as he stood on the ribbon strip of beach and helped the boat up; "I was beginning to think you were took with convulsions. Where's old Burke?"

"On his back there," said Messenger, springing to the sand, "and pretty bad at that. We'd better get him upstairs to begin on."

"By thunder!" exclaimed Kenner when he saw him, the bandage blood-covered, and the man groaning heavily. "What's he been at? I guess there's half of his features wanting. You've had a stick-up, then?"

"As you say," said Messenger, "but the news will wait; we must get him up first. One of you hand up the canvas while I hold him."

"Wal," said Kenner, "that's the Spanish way of drawing teeth, I calculate. Poor old Burke! it'll be many a day before he can show at a *soirée*, any way. Did you get all the stuff?"

"We left a keg," said Messenger quickly, "which you can fetch if you'll roll a dead man over. Have you seen anything of what's going on over yonder?"

"There's boats been by here three times in the hour, and the beach at the bottom of the bay is thick with men," replied Kenner. "I saw that by climbing up the rock there and holding on like a tenderfoot. I've no head for tall places."

"I'll look myself when the stuff's down," said Messenger; and with that the four of them hauled Burke to the ledge of rock, and, having given him some of the liquor, they bound up his face, using the sleeve of Kenner's shirt for the operation; and so they laid him upon the sail of the longboat; he yet groaning, though his pain seemed less. After that, it was half-an-hour's work to sink the gold in the creek and to store the few provisions they had taken from the Spaniards' boat; but the four worked with silent zeal, and Fisher not the least readily, since the rough philosophy he was master of told him again to go through with it.

When the bullion was quite sunk, and the longboat high in the water again, Messenger began to think of the scene being played in the bay without. Indeed, his attention was called to it before his own work was quite done, for the sky above the haven was suddenly lighted with a glowing red light, and this endured for some minutes before the four men were able to put the boat out and get to the bay. Kenner had reached the open, as he told them, by swarming along the face of the rock from ledge to ledge; but they rowed; and, having come into the bay, they saw at once from the loom of the land the striking development of the mystery. A great fire was now burning some half-a-mile from the opposite shore; and from the lapping tongues of red there stood up the masts of a fore-and-aft schooner. She had come ashore near the point; and was then surrounded by fishing-boats and small craft, whose crews seemed waiting patiently until the beacon of the sea should be engulfed. A mighty holocaust it was, the sparks leaping up on the breeze and falling hissing to the breakers; the smoke rolling in clouds of inky blackness away to the hills; the red light striking upon the waters and showing the environing fleet, whose fierce shouts of triumph the watchers heard all plainly. And, anon, there came a movement in the drama, for two long, black-hulled boats of men appeared suddenly near to the glowing schooner; and at the sight of them the small ships ran up sails or put out oars and went scudding away, some to the near shore, some towards the haven of the four, others to round the point and gain the village, which was at the back of the ravine in which the survivors of the *Semiramis* had come to hide.

As the boats hurried in flight Messenger instantly saw the danger.

"We must clear in," said he, "and risk the ship, too. If any of them strike our hole, there's not a man amongst us who'll see the morning; and the boat's the difficulty."

"Fix her up some hundred yards down the creek, and trust to luck," said Kenner. "We can swarm in as I did."

"That's what I mean to do," said the other; "but there's no time to lose. If my eyes aren't blinded by the fire, that lugger there is making straight for our place."

The whole bay was now full of small boats, luggers, yawls, cutters, which scuttled away briskly before the advent of the pursuers. The majority of them were soon lost to view in the darker shadows of the far land; but many belonged to the village on the other side of the promontory; and a few—these principally row-boats of a large size—were steering, as Messenger first had observed, straight for the creek wherein the gold had been cast. This, however, was a wrong impression, and was quickly corrected. Presently the helm of the lugger which threatened the four was put down; and the craft lay with its nose pointing almost to the south of the bay. At the same moment the high land, to which the new course shaped, was lighted with the flare of many torches; and these gave illumination enough for the observers to see a party of men on horseback riding upon the cliffs; and at the head of the party was a woman, who seemed to be commanding those who followed.

Now, before Messenger and the others had seen this, they had brought their own craft into a deep fjord of the cliff, some quarter of a mile below their own haven; but the change of the other's course reassured them, and when they had lain a long while during the passing of the two boats, and the gradual clearing of the bay, they rowed back to their place of camping, and made fast their craft in a corner of the pool, where it was safe from the view of all those who should not expressly seek it. Thus they reached the chamber of the rock, and the place where Burke was; and for the first time since sundown could think of rest.

It had been a night eventful enough to be called, then and after, the terrible night; yet, with all their fatigue and overwhelming weariness, the four could not sleep. Burke lay almost insensible and stupefied where they had first put him; but the others, huddling over their cold food, and weighed down with the hazards of the situation, had no minds but for the metaphorical morrow with its possibilities and its dangers. And until the dawn they planned and schemed; and at every swish of water below them they looked to see a man-of-war's boat enter the cove.

Of the four Kenner appeared to suffer the deepest depression. He had said little since he saw the party of horsemen upon the cliff and the woman riding at the head of them; but when dawn was near, and Fisher and the nigger were at length lying in a heavy sleep upon the rocks, he turned to Messenger and spoke openly of his fears.

"Prince," said he, "do you remember three months ago at Monaco?"

"Perfectly," replied the other.

"And the Spanish woman?"

"I seem to recall some of your vapourings in that direction," Messenger answered languidly.

"Call 'em what you like. I'm referring to the witch with the teeth set in her head like glass in a brick wall—the woman and the girl with the pretty face. You've a mind to recollect them, perhaps?"

"Why should I remember them?"

"Didn't the youngster say that he saw the girl when he went ashore the other day?"

"You didn't believe that story, surely?" asked Messenger.

"I guess I did; and I'll tell you right here that the woman who rode on the cliffs to-night should have been her mother."

"Should have been," said Messenger wearily; "how's that?"

"Because I know it! I can't tell you why, but I know it. Her name's the Countess Yvena, and I was with those who shot her husband in New Mexico."

The Prince, weary as he was, laughed outright at the story.

"Kenner," said he, "you were born a poet; you've got imagination. Now you speak of it, I remember your twaddle about having to meet her again, or something."

"That's what I know," said Kenner; "we'll meet again, and one of us will go under——"

"It's a fine tale, man," interrupted the Prince, "but you're wasting breath on it. Didn't we arrange an hour ago that you were to get away to Ferrol as soon as the dark and the cut-throats round here will let you."

"That's so," replied Kenner; "but I'll have to return."

"Well, what of that? Where does the woman come in? Besides, you're dreaming the whole thing. You don't mean to tell me seriously that the person we saw to-night is the one who ate oysters with her fingers in the gardens at Monaco three months ago?"

"Wal, you reassure a man. Like enough, the kid's story set me thinking of it, and I'm not myself——"

"Are any of us any better off?" asked the Prince. "It's the want of food and rest; and we're not likely to get much of either until you return. But we trust in you. As I said an hour ago, if you can, with the aid of money, reach Ferrol in a couple of days, you'll find an American Consul there. You won't forget that you wish to view the Basque provinces from the sea, and are seeking a yacht for that purpose. The smaller the ship you buy, the better afterwards. We'll run round to Lisbon in the guise of mere pleasure-seekers, and then send you back to London to buy a steamer. Whatever they're doing there now in the way of taking us, they'll never look for our return; and a little good disguise should make the matter as easy as shelling peas."

"What if you're took before I can get back here?"

"I don't foresee anything of that sort. Europe's ringing with the tale of this robbery, of course. You may be quite sure that we're wanted in every big city, and there's employment for all the detectives living, and more. It's true that we've had a bit of a brawl with the shoremen here, but I don't think we've been sighted by any in authority; and while that continues to be so we're safe. The sharpest detective living can't have looked for the wreck of the yacht. If I was figuring this thing out on shore, I should expect the man who ran a cargo such as we ran to have shaped either for Buenos Ayres or for Rio. They may have searched the Spanish coast—like enough the ironclad we saw yesterday was on that tack—but for our foundering, no, there will scarcely have been a man sharp enough to have foreseen that."

"Wal," said Kenner, "you've hitched on to reason, and I'd shout glory with you if it wasn't for this notion of the woman which sticks in my head. Anyway, I start to-morrow night, and if I come back with a ship you'll have nothing agen me. What I'm thinking of now is Burke."

"You're wasting time; he's a carcase like flint, and the heart of a bull. Three days should see him well; but come and look at him."

Upon this they both went to the place where the skipper was lying, and found him to be still feverish, but cooler, while he slept more restfully. When they had reassured themselves thus, the two, dawn having fully come, gave way to their fatigue, and making what beds they could upon the hard rock, they fell to slumber at once, and did not awake for many hours.

But on the following night, at the first fall of darkness, they put Kenner ashore some miles down the coast, and he, armed abundantly with sovereigns and carrying only his revolver, struck inland to gain the high road to Ferrol. And with him he took all the hope of the four that remained about the treasure, for upon his safety depended not only their success but their very lives.

CHAPTER XIX.

THE SECOND WRECKING.

SEVEN days after the departure of Kenner from the haven, the camp of the four left upon the coast presented a sorry spectacle. Much of the food had already been consumed, and there remained little but biscuit and potatoes, and the spirit taken from the yacht and the locker of the longboat; but the more part of the men's suffering was the result of the ceaseless watching and the nervous unrest which were the outcome of the situation. From the beginning Messenger had forbidden all prospecting; and had sunk the boat in the pool for their greater security. The camp, too, was now pitched some hundred yards farther up the path which led through the cañon; a mighty convenient place having been found in one of the offshoots, which led into a little cavern of the cliff; from whose roof the stalactites were depending in many shapes. Here boulders were rolled to form a barrier; and there being a natural chimney at the far end of the refuge, the men even ventured upon a fire, whereat they cooked the potatoes, and boiled their water in an ammunition case, which leaked abundantly, yet served their purpose. They had become, by this time, accustomed to the life; and had there been a plenitude of food, would have suffered little from exposure in a climate where heat was the enemy, and the sun was welcomed chiefly at the setting.

Burke, the skipper, had by this time recovered almost completely from his wound. His gigantic constitution had helped him where other men would have died without a struggle; and, though his face was yet bound up (and, as it proved, was horribly scarred), he continued to possess some of his old recklessness, and the best part of his characteristic profanity. Yet it was tedious, this watching and waiting, suspense and hope, fear and desperation; nor had the four any topic of conversation but such questions as "Where's Kenner now? Has he put to sea yet, do you think? Is he taken?"

I have said that the men lay hid in this cavernous concealment; but it is not to be thought that they had no sort of knowledge of that which was passing in the bay without. Every morning after the first meal, and again before sundown, Messenger and Fisher left the cave, and, striking through an exceeding narrow path they had discovered some fifty yards higher up the ravine, they climbed, with little difficulty, to a natural window in the face of the cliff; and there had the bay spread below them, and could see to the distant mountains of Asturia, with the whole panorama of hill and forest and luxurious wooded plain intervening. For the greater part of the day the bay itself lacked even the ornament of a single ship; but oftentimes, towards the setting of the sun, fishing-luggers were seen on the horizon, and a few passed in to the anchorage of the shallows. Yet no man showed himself upon the beach, and the men lived in a wild and unspeakable solitude, which almost magnified their fears.

Upon the fourth evening, and again upon the fifth, after Kenner's going, the wind blew savagely from the north-west, sending long white-topped breakers into the bay; and the air being deliciously fresh at the window of watching, Messenger and the lad sat there long, not a little surprised at the sights they saw upon the shore when dark had come— and the gale rose with a thunder of noise and a dismal riot of wind at the flow of the tide. On both these nights, no sooner was the day done than a clear white light, burning, apparently, from some boat moored in the offing, shone with great power at intervals of a minute; and continued thus to stand as a signal for many hours. On the second night, however, when the strange lantern had burned for no more than ten minutes, a gun-shot was fired from the shore, and the light was extinguished. At a later hour, when the moon struggled through the halo of cloud and showed the face of the country, Fisher pointed out that the woman who had been at the head of the horsemen three nights gone was again riding, but this time unattended, upon the cliffs; and when Messenger observed her he recalled with some force Kenner's fears and his surmises.

"Hal," said he, "when you came across the girl in the hills the other day did you really think you had seen her before?"

"I am sure of it: and she told me so," replied Fisher. "She was the girl who used to be with the woman we called the Spanish witch."

"That's odd—remarkably odd," said the other, next. "I remember that the fellow of our hotel declared the Spanish woman to be a wrecker with a castle somewhere upon the northern shore of Spain. It would be almost grotesque to think he spoke the truth"

Fisher shrugged his shoulders. Since the day of the last visit to the wreck, he had betrayed little enthusiasm in anything. The hinges of his friendship still worked, but stiffly; and though the personal force of Messenger yet exercised a certain power, it was not the power of the old time. And this change did not in any way escape the man. He had looked for something of the sort; but had thought to tide it over by pleasantry and artifice. Now, however, when it became clear that the lad distrusted him wholly, he became irritable and reserved with him.

"Come," said he, "you're a lively companion, I must say. What's the matter with you?"

"I was thinking of the men in the cabin," replied Fisher.

"Well, and what of them? Surely you didn't look for me to leave half a dozen kegs of gold, entrusted to my solemn care by those that have confidence in me, to the first knaves who try and steal it."

"Not at all," said Fisher, trying to be unconvinced.

"Then what are you pulling a long face about? They tried to cut our throats, and we cut theirs. Perhaps you think we should now be under the sea, and they spending our money ashore?"

"Your money?" asked Fisher with emphasis.

Messenger turned upon him a look which might have withered a stouter than the lad.

"It's a nice question to ask a friend," said he.

Fisher was abashed of his own suspicion.

"Indeed," cried he, "I'd gladly think all that's good of you."

Messenger turned away in pretended anger.

"Hal," said he, after a pause, "when we come ashore safely with this money you shall have the whole tale. If you can't trust me until then, go your way, and I'll go mine. I've stood without friends before; I can stand again."

"Oh," said Fisher, whose heart was wrung boyishly, "it will never be that, Prince. Heaven knows there's little I wouldn't do for you; and I can never tell how much you've done for me."

"All I ask is your friendship, as it was, and your trust," said Messenger, who aped the sorrow of suspicion to perfection; "your trust until I can repay you with my story."

"You're very good to me," said Fisher; "and the only one that's ever been so."

Thus was the breach in some measure temporarily hidden, and upon the seventh night, there having been a stiff gale all day, the whole party were expecting the return of Kenner with a keen hope; and talked of it huddled round the puny fire of logs in their camp. They had had little food for some hours; and at Burke's miserable cry for meat they had determined upon a sortie at midnight, whatever might be the risk. The plan, however, was never perfected, for at the hour of nine, as they judged, there was a booming of a gun heard even in the cave, and the two ran quickly up to the window of the cliff, and there saw a scene which had for them a sharp significance.

Upon a spot not three hundred yards removed from the shallows whereon the schooner had burned, a long, black coasting-steamer lay plain to be seen, with the surf thundering upon her; and the light of the moon being rich and full, it was even possible to perceive the crew huddled in her stern, yet grievously washed by the floods of water which swept her. That, however, which was by far the more engrossing spectacle to Messenger was the sudden activity which the striking of this ship produced upon the shore; for, no sooner had she fired a second gun than a whole fleet of boats seemed to shoot mysteriously from the high cliffs at the neck of the bay and to be rowed with uncommon vigour towards the wreck. And before you could tell it, the crews of these were swarming up to the poop of the beaten vessel, and it was possible to see the fierce fight for foothold which they made; many a man going overboard to the rolling swell, and many a one falling before the slash of knives and cudgels. But anon the attackers got full possession of the deck, and began to bundle out plunder of all sorts into the boats below, which were handled with consummate skill. And this occupation continued until a gun-shot from the shore recalled the men from their work, and they returned to a place upon the beach where many torches awaited them, and a throng of men had gathered.

To the two watching at the window, this business was an amazing revelation. Messenger himself, gripped by the most profound gloom, did not speak a word during the whole of it; but when the lights upon the foreshore had disappeared, he turned to Fisher and said—

"That's an amazing spectacle yonder."

"I'm of your opinion," said Fisher.

"And the tale of the Spanish woman at Monaco was true—she's a wrecker. Well, she must be a cute woman, and the coast-guard here must be a fine service—to make money in."

"I can hardly believe it," said Fisher, "though I've seen it with my own eyes."

."That I understand," said Messenger. "The

whole thing has come upon me like a thunderclap. Why, look at it; we, who thought ourselves just about a hundred miles from anywhere, have plumped down upon a community of cut-throats, whose number it would be a waste of time to calculate. Don't you see that if one of these men tracked us we shouldn't have ten minutes to live?"

"Would they be likely to guess about the bullion?" asked Fisher speculatively.

"Guess about it? What nonsense! Of course they would. The woman plays a double part. I can see the whole of it. She's got a gang round her here who deal with ships, and she spends the profits at Monaco. That's an idea to dream of, my boy; it's a stupendous idea. If I'd have met her about twenty years ago, we might have made what the society papers call a pretty couple."

He had dropped into satire for a moment; but his mood quickly turned to one of great seriousness.

"Hal," said he, as they climbed down from the window of rock, "there's to be little sleep for us to-night. It's true we should look for Kenner now, but who can say whether he's afloat or ashore, alive or dead? As there may be days to wait, I want to know where the path which runs through the cliff leads to. Did you notice that all the boats shot out from the shore not a mile below us? Well, if there's a camp there, the road, which we know nothing about, may bring us to it; and in that case we might have a visit before morning. I dare not even think what they would do if they learnt about the wreck."

"Is there time to get away with the gold now?" said Fisher.

"No, I don't think so; it seems to me that we ran an almighty risk every time we put the boat out, though we didn't know it. Luck has been with us so far; we must trust to it a little longer."

They had now come to the cave again, and found Burke and the negro fast asleep. Embers of the wood glowed upon the rock; but these they doused, and, having made everything trim for concealment, they took their pistols, a length of rope, and some spirit in one of the flasks, and set out quickly upon their journey.

CHAPTER XX.

THE MAN BY THE DOOR.

THE night was one of wind and storm, the sky being scoured by cumulose clouds which permitted the moon's light but at intervals. Blasts whistled dismally through the gullies of the hills. During the first stage of the journey, the path of the ravine which the man and the lad trod continued as a parallel to the sea; but at the distance of a third part of a mile or less from the camp there was a sharp turn of it; and there a more open way, bearing evidences of human handiwork, rose with an easy gradient towards the highland. The new road had a width of six feet even at the narrows of it, and was good to walk upon, though strewn with boulders and often wet with the flashing cascades which gushed from the softer rock. As for the walls, they, in the moments when a glow of the moon's rays struck down into the chasm, shone with the fire of jasper and of quartz and of ore of antimony; and through the canopy of peaks the stars were seen clothed with an infinite brilliance and beauty.

I have said that the broader path appeared at the

outset to lead to the highland and away from the sea, but a longer exploration of it disclosed many windings and labyrinthic passages; so that the two presently lost knowledge of their situation, or of the direction in which the way was carrying them. They now found it necessary to bring great caution to the work, more especially in the intervals when the path lay hid in utter darkness; and often they stood quite still to listen for the sound of voices or of others moving; but the place was possessed of a great silence, broken only by the sough of the wind and the splash of the water where the mountain streams fell toward the bay.

It must have been at a distance of at least a mile from the haven that the first plain change in the nature of the path was manifest. At this point, there was a great increase of its steepness, the gradient being so sharp that it was a labour to walk upright; and there were even rugged steps which bore the stamp of antiquity upon them; and were so hid with rocks and stones that the possibility of their having been in common use was out of the question. The ravine itself was now comparatively shallow, the walls being nowhere more than twenty or thirty feet in height, and they fell back so much at their summits that the shrubs and trees of the higher plain were clearly visible; and this new state was unaltered until, at last, the path ended in a great door of wood, upon the top of which a row of iron spikes was set.

At the foot of the door Messenger stopped, and, motioning to Fisher to crouch down, he listened with a strained ear for some minutes. In this place, as lower in the gully, there was singing of wind, which seemed almost to cry in the hills; but the gale was intermittent, and when both of them had listened patiently for more than a quarter of an hour the sound of dipping oars came up as from some deep chasm behind the barrier. It was a momentary sound, and was lost again almost as they heard it; yet its import seemed considerable, and was deepened at another fall of the blast, in which the crying of men one to the other was unmistakably audible.

"Hark!" said Messenger in a whisper: "could that be anything else but a man hailing from a boat? We appear to have come upon a colony."

"I wonder what's behind the door?" asked Fisher naturally.

"I'll tell you in five minutes," said the other, "if it's to be told at all. Give me a back while I shin up the place here."

It was no very difficult work to obtain foothold on the rock at the side of the decaying gate; and when the man had once come within reach of the spikes, he held to them easily, standing with one foot upon a natural ledge, and using a loop of the rope hitched over the iron as a support for the other. But Fisher stood below, and, when Messenger did not speak for many minutes, he began to conclude that he had fathomed the secret of the voices.

"Prince," asked he at length, in a whisper which was half a shout, " can you see anything ? "

" Not so loud ! " replied the other, bending down to answer. " I think there are men below, but I'll tell you presently. Take another twist with the rope and pull yourself up. That's it ! Now, what do you make of it ? "

Fisher was then beside him, placed much as he was, but at the opposite post of the gate. At the first glance he could see little beyond the spikes, for the darkness was intense, and a great wall of cliff loomed up at a distance of some fifty yards from their standing-place; but, when the bank of cloud passed off the face of the moon, the whole scene was illumined sharply. It was now clear that their path was a disused one, but formerly had led unchecked to a great creek of the sea; and the two were now looking down to this creek, but from a vast height, since the path broke into the northern wall of the fjord almost at its summit. Thus it was that they saw, both above and below their standing-place, the glow of light upon a lagoon-like basin of water; but directly beneath them the view downwards was obstructed by a projecting roof, as of some building hugging to the very sides of the rock; and the stone parapet of this was not more than ten feet below them.

I, when reading the papers which deal with these moments of this episode, have often thought that the future of the men who survived the *Semiramis* might have been different had Messenger quieted the curiosity which led him to cross the gate. If the projection of the roof had permitted him to see straight down into the creek, there can be no doubt that he had returned immediately to the haven, and rested there until Kenner's coming was a fact, or at least until there had been news of him; but, being unable to see more than deeply-fissured walls of whitish rock and the top of a building of stone, he confessed that he felt no surer of the situation than he did at the outset, and the needs of a reconnoitre compelled him to go on. And with this intention he turned to Fisher; but a new sound of voices came up to them suddenly from the chasm; and at this he dropped from his position, and said—

"That decides it; we are going over to inspect. Send down the rope with a loop in it, and leave it there to get back quickly if there's need; but you must tread like a cat, and for the life of you don't speak!"

"It's a big risk," exclaimed Fisher, whose foresight in this matter was sharper than the other's, and who feared exceedingly. But the man was impatient.

"There's no risk if you do exactly as I do," said he. "Give me your end of the rope, and help me up again."

He was at the gate again with this, hitching the line to a whole spike; and when he had forced two others from their place—for the gate was exceeding rotten—he swung himself lightly down, and gave a sign to the lad that he should come upon the parapet. Fisher followed him nimbly, and the two quickly stood together upon the roof, and looked down sheer to the tremendous depths below.

The scene then spread below them was one so weird and so strange that they may well have contemplated it in silence for many minutes. There was, as they had thought, a vast chasm with a lake of water at the foot of it; but it's depth, when thus looked down upon, seemed infinitely beyond anything they had anticipated; and the uprising walls of rock presented sheer precipices, which were amazing in their grandeur and their height. Yet was this work of Nature of poor interest for them by the side of the human activity to be observed below. At the landward end of the creek, where there was the mouth of a tunnel leading, as they supposed, from the lagoon into the very heart of the cliff, a fleet of rowboats and of luggers lay moored; and the crews passed to and fro to narrow and wharf-like ledges upon either side of the great orifice, which was all lit up by the flare of torches, and echoing with the hailing of seamen and the buzz of voices. What with the flickering light upon the dark water, and the reek of the smoke, and the sight of savage faces, and the shout of orders, and the forbidding aspect of the vast passage, the whole came upon the two men watching like a revelation; and they lay spellbound and speechless, unable to turn back for very curiosity, yet afraid almost to move, lest a false step should cost them their lives.

They were (as I say) perched upon the roof of a stone building, encased in the very side of the cliff; but they perceived, when they looked from this, that a comparatively wide path ran along the side of the ravine some thirty feet below them, and the house, or whatever it was, upon which they stood had a frontage to the path; yet from its dilapidation they judged that it was now not used, and that thus their position was less dangerous than they had at first thought. So plain was this at last that Messenger began boldly to crawl the whole length of the parapet; and when he had come to the far end, he, crouching down very close upon the stone, beckoned the lad to follow him; and they stood together at last by a trap-door, half lifted from its resting-place; and so permitting them, when the light was good enough, to see the interior of the room below them. But they beheld only a windowless and reeking chamber, barred, it is true, against egress with stout iron bars, yet having its door open and crying upon its hinges; and they were about to turn away when Fisher's quick eyes discovered that which they had not seen, but which conveyed so dismal a warning.

"Look," said he, "I could swear that a man lay in the corner by the door."

"I can see nothing," said Messenger; "you're discovering the shadow of the trap."

"No, it isn't that; shift the trap gently, and you'll see it for yourself."

They moved the wooden lid of the aperture, and then the sight was plain. A body lay upon the floor —across the very threshold, in fact—but it was the body of a dead man; and when the light was full enough they saw that the man was Parker, the humble mate of the *Semiramis*.

"Good God!" said Messenger, "it's the mate; how did he get into this hole?"

"He must have been saved from the ship," said Fisher. "Poor old Parker: he was one of the few decent ones among them."

"Well," said the man; "he'll want decent burial, any way; and I'll tell you that it's just about time we went back again."

"As you say," said Fisher, and at that he turned to crawl back from the place; but the movement was a clumsy one, and, striking the wooden trap-door with his arm, he sent it clattering and whirling to the water below. No sooner had it fallen than a shout went up from the depths, and the two knew how great their folly had been; for while they talked, dawn had come, and their figures were observed by the horde below, who yelled with ferocity at the very sight of them.

CHAPTER XXI.

FLIGHT TO THE SEA.

WHILE he stood, no longer crouching, but upright with defiance of the danger, Messenger took a swift survey of his environment. Immediately above him the rock rose to a height of thirty feet, but with a sheer face which forbade any attempt to swarm it; in front was the abyss, with a throng of men at the bottom of it, gesticulating and roaring like wolves who hunger. His first thought, naturally, was against flight by the ravine leading to the haven, lest the course should disclose their hiding-place; but, failing this, there was only the path twenty feet below, and whether or no this would, even could they reach it, bring them to the sea he knew not. A rifle shot, which rang past his head and struck the rock with a sharp "ping," decided him.

"It must be the gate or nothing," said he; "and we'll have to run for it when we get down. Over you go, Hal, or they'll be hitting you."

The fear of the latter words was not justified. The projection of the roof put the men momentarily out of sight; and Fisher was in comparative security when he grasped the rope to pull himself up. One mighty haul he gave with his brawny arms, but not a second; for the spike had cut the strands of the line; and the lad rolled upon his back with a short length of it still in his hands.

In the face of this new disaster the two, for the moment, stood without idea or speech. So steep, indeed, so overhanging was the rock on the hither side of the gate, that it was idle even to venture the effort of climbing it; and no words from one man to the other were needed to express the whole of the hazard. There it was in all its nakedness. Before them was the rock; below them was the chasm; and, as they soon learned, there were men coming up the goat-path towards the house upon whose roof they stood. But at this Messenger began to run distractedly up and down the place again; and, as soon as he showed himself, another bullet struck against the parapet; and the howls of the savage horde were louder and more fierce.

Now, at this supremity of the crisis, and when two of the men running upon the path were within fifty paces of the stone house, but fortunately bearing no arms, Messenger looked up at the cliff above the end of the building which was furthest from the gate, and saw that it was less steep than the precipice which forbade his return to the haven. At any other time he would have deemed the man who had attempted to climb it nothing less than a lunatic; but now, with a desperation which was of the position, he clutched at this straw and dared the hazard.

"Hal," said he, "I'm going up the cliff there: will you come?"

"I'll try," said Fisher laconically; but the Prince gave him no opportunity for answer. He had already sprung up at the rock, clutching it with a fierce, nervous grip, and pulling himself from bush to bush with a frenzy which reckoned with no danger and was swift in its success. Indeed, before the lad himself could move, the other was half way to the summit, hanging, as it seemed, against the perpendicular face of the rock, and above a precipice two hundred feet in depth; and still he went on where one would have said no man could go—on where a false step would have sent him reeling down to death upon the stones below—and Fisher's head whirled at the sight, and he declared to himself that he could not follow, though his life hung upon the venture.

For my own part, I am led to believe that the younger man would never have dared this flight had it not been for the appearance of one of the Spaniards at the trap-door in the roof. Just as the lad was in the throes of his hesitation, and stood trembling with his doubt, the head of a huge shoreman came up through the aperture; and a deep exclamation burst from the fellow when he saw his prey. But Fisher was prompted only to action; and now, awake to the peril, he took a running kick at the head, and, as the Spaniard withdrew it, shouting horribly with his pain, the lad put his foot upon a protuberance of the rock and began boldly to climb it.

For the first few steps the way was easy, yet carried him from the shelter of the intervening roof, so that, had he cared to look, his eyes could have fathomed the whole depth of the chasm. But when, working from ledge to ledge until he had mounted some twenty feet of the forty, he came of a sudden to a bulging shelf which forced the upper part of his body from the rock, he thought that he must let go; and he seemed in his mind already to be flying through the air and waiting the final shock of death. He had hoped that the strip of path running to the stone house would have hid the whole of the ravine's depth from him; but it was cut in this place under a projection of the cliff, and did not help him. And now he came to a ledge where he could neither go on nor retrace his steps; and as he held to a branch of a bush which began to tremble at its roots, he knew that if he moved so much as a foot he would fall inevitably. In this terror he closed his eyes, and, with his head singing as a sick man's, he waited for the end—and was very near to death when something hard struck him upon the arm, and he looked up, to see a short bar of iron with a rope swinging before him. At this he clutched, and three minutes after he was upon the bank above, lying flat and feeling the ground with his hands to be sure that fancy had not cheated him.

"I'll give you a minute to get your head, and no

"AT THIS HE CLUTCHED" (*p.* 224).

more," said Messenger, who bent over him. "You should send a letter of thanks to the woman who owns this place for roping in the cliff with lines and posts. I pulled the last post up, and let the cord swing down to you. But we'll have to run for it: I can see men moving in the woods already."

Fisher sat up at the last words and perceived that they were upon the sward of a great park, with the cliffs of the sea stretching upon their right hand, but bordered thickly with clumps of pines; while greater woods, principally of chestnut-trees, stood out upon their left. Between the coverts there was a great open space of grass; and behind them, at the distance of a third of a mile, the castle, which they had seen from the other bay, shone brightly in the first light of the sun. It was from a wood which ran almost to the very door of this rugged building that twenty or more men now appeared, shouting to the two, and running hard across the great green, which had the smoothness of a lawn.

"Come," said Messenger, when the men stood out plain to their sight, "I was something of a runner at Cambridge, and I know you are. You've got to do a mile now, and under 'five;' I'll trouble you to make the pace."

"I'll make it fast enough for a Spaniard, any way," said Fisher, as he started; and for the next ten minutes the men ran like hares, hearing wild shouts behind them, but no reports of guns. When at length they came to the woods, the pursuing party was two-thirds of a mile away; but Messenger still held on, forcing his way through untrodden brushwood and thick coverts of thorns, until at last they came within view of the sea, and both stood to pant like horses that have run a race. Then they doubled back through the wood, but kept parallel with the shore, until at last they plunged into the dry bed of that which was never more than a rivulet; and finding it roofed with a thick canopy of leaves, they followed its course for some quarter of a mile. The gully carried them at length to a deeper pit, all fenced about with shrubs and saplings, and here they lay listening to distant shouting in the thickets, and to the call of men to men for directions or for orders.

During the whole of the heat of the mid-day hour, and on through the terrible afternoon, the two lay in their place of concealment, the leaves thick above them, their bodies flat upon the ground, as the bodies of scouts who watch. Often they heard the voices of men; and the crackling of the brushwood and the bramble about spoke of the continuance of the search; but in the later afternoon the sounds ceased, and thence onward a rustling of aspens and the music of leaves alone disturbed the silence of the woodland.

It must have been very near to the hour of nine o'clock before Messenger, being well assured that the wood immediately about them was free of men, ventured to stand up and take a swift survey of his environment. Twilight had then almost given place to the dark of night; the sky was wanting clouds, and tree and wood and hill-land stood plain to be seen; there was a stillness of the air which gave to every sound, even of an insect buzzing or a bat winging, a distinctness of poor omen to the two who lay hid. Yet the time for action had come; nor could it be delayed any longer, as both of them knew.

"Hal," whispered Messenger, when he had crawled once right round the pit, "I've lost my bearings altogether, man. There's north right between the thickets yonder, and the cove should lie a little to the east of it—but how we're to find a path, God knows."

"And the place will swarm with men," said Fisher.

"Of course, if they haven't thought better of it and gone to bed. But that's to be learnt. Do you see the hill with the big furze bush on the crest of it? I'm going as near to the top of that as I can get without drawing shot. While I'm gone, you crawl up to the green between the thickets there, and use your eyes for all you're worth. But you won't forget that if you're seen, you may as well say your prayers at once."

"How long shall you be gone?" asked Fisher, with a disregard to the question which showed that he was aware of its importance.

"Just as short a time as will tell me if I sleep here to-night or alongside old Burke."

"And if men should sight us?"

"Why, just run for it. A shot would bring a

regiment down on us. You must use your wits, man; you can't be laying it down like lines upon a plan. But I'm hoping the road's clear."

All this he said in whisper, and at the last word he threw himself flat again, and began to crawl through the brushwood with a supple cleverness which was wonderful. But Fisher did not wait to watch his path, seeking to imitate his litheness, and to reach the high thickets which lay to the north of the stream's bed. His was the fairer work, for he passed through a plantation of young trees which gave shelter to his movements, and the grass below him was almost free of briar. Yet he went with infinite caution, and his heart quaked at every snap of crag or rustle of leaf. When at the last he had come to the summit of the wooded hill, he felt his face wet with perspiration; and he lay for many minutes fighting for his breath before he looked out upon the scene below him.

It was as he had thought. From the place by the thicket there was view of the sea, then shining with silvery light, and unruffled; but the beach was not to be observed. And the lower lands around, both the park and the woods bordering upon it, were very clearly visible, no men being about them, nor any sign of watch or camp. And this was so plain that he had intention immediately to return to the place of the pit, when the sudden flash of a light between the trees compelled him to throw himself down once more, and to watch the path of the lantern (for so he judged it to be) with all the fear and expectancy he had known so often since the stranding of the yacht.

Whence came the light? By whom was it carried? An older man than he would have said that one of low stature bore it, since it swung but a handsbreadth from the ground; and in like manner it was plain that whoever carried the lantern had no thought of concealment, but advanced quickly through the thicket, as the dancing light gave witness. Presently, the rays went darting here and there upon fern and flower with lurches, which told that the one who used it ran; and there was much crushing of the dead leaves, and the sound of quick breathing. But the lad listening lay closer than ever at this; and as the light steps were more clearly audible, it seemed to him that by a miracle alone could he escape observation and all that must accompany it.

When the lad was wondering, as we wonder in danger, where he would be, and under what conditions, in an hour's time, the lantern suddenly cast an aureola about him; and in the shadow he saw the face and figure of the girl of Monaco. She was passing swiftly, a mantilla half hiding her pretty head, her dress drawn up about her knees, in her right hand a whip, the great Dane at her heels—but at the lad's word, which he could not hold back, she stopped of a sudden, and thus they stood face to face. For a long time she did not speak, but the colour heightened upon her cheek as she saw upon whom she had come, and the lace upon her breast rose and fell while she listened to his rapid words.

"I saw your light," said Fisher bluntly, assuming that she knew of his situation, "and feared that the gang was upon us again. My friend and I are lying down in the brushwood yonder, but we are nearly dead with fatigue and want of food. If you could show us a safe road to the shore, I could not thank you enough."

They stood, as I have said, face to face, the boy and the girl; and yet there was between them that understanding which flashes up instinctively in the young day of life; and they knew that words were not wanting upon the seal of their confidence. He, for his part, put his safety into her hands as readily as he would have put it into the hands of one he had known since childhood; and when she answered him, she did so without any fear or pretence of ignorance.

"I know all your story," said she. "They were saying at the house that you had gone into the woods by the other bay, and they are searching for you there. But I saw you come here from my window this morning, and I waited for the dark to help you. They are still watching upon the beach, but that is a mile from here."

She extinguished the lantern with her words, but not before he had asked her—

"Why do you do this for us?"

"I do it for you," she replied quite simply; "you

cannot understand, but I have never had a friend. My own people are a shame to me. My life is all loneliness. God only knows what it is——"

She spoke with such an infinite tenderness that Fisher caught her hand in his, and held it to his lips; and the touch of it sent him trembling.

"Would to God I could repay you," said he, "but I have nothing to offer but my gratitude, and what that is words could not tell you. I shall remember it to my last day——"

"And I shall remember you," said she, still permitting him to hold her; "I could never forget—you have given me happiness, and I have known so little."

Her note of sorrow struck in the lad a whole chord of fine chivalry. Standing as he did with her hand in his, and her hot breath upon his cheeks, almost feeling the rapid beating of her heart as she pressed against him, looking down into eyes that glowed with Southern passion, he vowed that he would return again whatever lot fate put upon him; and telling her this, regardless of time or place, he of a sudden drew her yet closer to him, and their lips met in the first kiss he had ever put upon the lips of woman. And for long moments she clung to him with tears upon her cheeks, and gladness at her heart, while the fire-flies played and the leaves trembled in the first flush of a warm breeze, and the woods were still in all the beauty of a summer's night.

The moment was long drawn, yet she, disengaging

herself from his embrace, was the first to come to her senses.

"We are both forgetting," said she; "and we stand where we must not forget. I am going to lead you through the private garden to the shore. I can do no more, and if the men return from the other end of the bay, it may only be leading you to danger. But it is all I can do."

"I am sure of it," said Fisher, "and we must take our chance. I shall tell Messenger all you have done."

"Indeed no," said she, "it was done for you. If you do not forget, that is all I ask."

There was no need for his answer. Yet he vowed again and again, as men vow, that he would never forget, and that he would come again to thank her, as he could not thank her then. Thus, hand in hand, they crept towards the hill whereon Messenger's watch had been, and to him it seemed that he told her the history of his life, and that he had found one who had caused a whole world of dreams to open before him enchantingly. But she, going on with quick steps, led him at last to the hill, and to the man who was already coming towards the thicket for an understanding of the delay.

"Well," said Messenger, observing the two, "you appear to be occupied. Is this the young lady you spoke of a week ago?"

"Yes," said Fisher simply; "this is the second time she has done us a service. She has just promised to take us through the private garden to the beach, which she thinks is free of men."

The Prince, looking upon the pair, did not even ask himself is it safe to go? He had reckoned up the chances at a thought, as the lad and the Spanish girl came towards him; and now he only thanked her with that infinite courtesy he was master of at any moment. But this being done, she led them quickly through the nearer of the woods until they came to a great wall of stone; and in this she unlocked a great iron door, and so they passed through a garden in which there were many arbours and fountains, until they stood at the summit of a rough flight of stone stairs; and here she left them before the man could speak another word to her, or the lad could touch her hand again.

The steps brought them upon the beach, which they found quite deserted; but walking quickly towards their own haven, as they judged, they presently saw the dark shape of a ship's boat; and they observed instantly that it was the longboat, in which the nigger, Joe, rowed, and Burke sat at the tiller.

At this sight, the fact being clear beyond dispute, Messenger stood quite still, and stamped angrily with his foot upon the sand.

"Curse them!" said he; "they're showing full in the light!" with this he began to run along the shore; and the skipper, seeing him, gave a low whistle and put the boat's head towards the beach. She touched a moment later; but, as the four greeted each other, a great shout rose up from the sand, and a horde of men, swarming fiercely about the party, had laid the whole of them flat upon their backs and bound them before they realised even whence the attack came.

CHAPTER XXII.

THE HALL OF FOUNTAINS.

WHEN the work was done, and the four Englishmen lay upon the beach, stiff with the ropes which bound them, the Spaniards, who had achieved such a quick capture, began to display their exultation with deep guttural cries. Some stood above the captives and uttered wild and shrill exclamations for several minutes; others ran along the beach calling loudly to their fellows on the cliffs above that the work was done; others, again, brought torches, which they thrust almost into the faces of the prisoners under the pretence of examining them. Nor was the band lacking the picturesque—numbering, as Messenger computed, at least thirty men, all armed with the cuchillo and with muskets, and clothed in garments which represented at once the tawdry splendour of the Southern taste and the warmer fashion of the mountain country. Here were rateros, in the gaudy cloaks of the Iberian; hulking seamen, in long mantles of rich and faded silk; bearded men, whose sashes shone with hues of intense red and aggressive yellow; swarthy Galicians, in the black zamarra;

simple peasants, who capered in the torch-light; even boys, who yodled at the victory. And for a long space they kept up the tow-row and the din, and threatened the bound men with their knives or their cudgels.

That there was any merit in the capture is not to be conceded. Messenger's own record, from which this present account is chiefly written, establishes the simplicity of it. "I lay it," says he, "entirely to my own folly in getting upon the roof of the rock-house that we were taken. Certainly, the girl had no hand in it. The Spaniards must have watched for us upon the shore all day, and Burke's madness in coming out of the haven gave them the clue they waited for. When they did spring upon us, it was with the dash of a cavalry-charge. I had three men upon my back and three at my throat before I could put a hand upon my pistol; and scarce had I touched the floor, when a fellow whipped a slip-knot round my arms, and pinned them so that the rope cut my flesh."

The record of the others gives a like account. And in one matter, at any rate, their thoughts were very similar. That this was the supremity of their disaster was as plain to them as the faces of the swarthy horde who gibbered upon the sand; but whether the Spaniards had actually come upon the gold—or, indeed, knew anything of its history—they could not tell. It was sufficient for them that they were thus in the hands of a babbling crew who seemed to restrain themselves from immediate murder with personal pain; and they could only conclude, with overwhelming bitterness, that chance had written for them this blunt termination of their emprise, and that they amongst them would be lucky who lived to see another sun.

As the moments passed, this gloomy thought became their only one in the presence of the immediate danger from the exulting Spaniards. Some of these, in the play of their humour, now began to thrash the bodies of the bound with their knotted sticks; others thrust their torches very near to the faces of the prone men; or threatened them with their cuchillos. It is scarce possible, in fact, to believe that the end of the four would not have come quickly had there not been the intervention of one in authority, a giant of a man, in a capa edged with fur and a fine sombrero; at the sound of whose voice the mob fell back and stood silent. But he, coming up to Messenger and making him a profound bow, seemed to be finding apology; and, when he had doffed his hat many times, he turned about and spoke to a man at his elbow, and, at that, the cords which held the necks and the ankles of the captives were cut, and the four of them were lifted into two boats which had been rowed to the sand during the *mêlée*.

The first of these, a pretty craft finished like a yacht's boat, took Messenger and Fisher; the second, a plainer ship, but one holding at least twenty men, had Burke and the nigger. And the boats being thus laden, the Spaniards rowed quickly up the bay, and Messenger's hope sank low when he observed that their course was for the lagoon he had fled from in the morning, and that the men who had debouched upon them were also those who had cried to one another in the door of the tunnel.

During this short voyage the boat which carried Burke fell rapidly behind the lighter craft wherein Messenger was, he sitting at the stern with the big man beside him, and Fisher lying, in the greatest state of fear he had ever known, at the bows. Both of them now had the shackles of the rope only upon their hands; yet thought of any attempt to turn the situation by leaping from the boat was out of their minds; and would, at the best, have been idle thought. As for the older man, his quick-scheming mind already ran upon a dozen ways and means; yet he could shape nothing until time should tell him more explicitly how the position lay; and, in the expectation of light, he turned to the Spaniard and asked him in French—

"Where are you taking us?"

"Sabe Dios, quien sabe," replied the fellow stoically.

Messenger, not having a phrase of Spanish to understand the sarcasm, ventured the thing again; this time in English.

"Do you belong to the place on the hill?"

The man responded with a "Perdone, señor," and another smile, showing, had there been light by which to see them, a fine row of brown teeth. Then he pointed with abundant gesticulation towards the haven; and seemed to wish to say that the position of the prisoners caused suffering to himself. But Messenger, believing that he was understood, went on with his talk.

"You seem to have a pretty crew of vagabonds at your beck and call," said he. "But this is going to cost you dear. We're expecting a ship from Ferrol to-morrow, and the English consul there will know where to look for us. You play a dangerous game!"

To his vast surprise the Spaniard laughed right out at this remark.

"Possibly," said he, in the English of the Palais Royal—"possibly; but we play him with the pistol in the pocket, señor. Your pardon, I speak what the English call the warning—you be exhorted of me and take him."

"Oh, then, you're the chief," said Messenger, looking at him closely, "and the owner of the place, I presume?"

"It is mine, and yet, as you speak, it is not mine. I serve my mistress there are thirty years; I will serve her thirty more—ojala!"

"Are we going to her now?"

"No, se sabe. I tell you in the come-and-by" (he meant the by-and-by). "I am but the servant; the servant cannot make speak when the mistress does not speak—not at all, by no means!"

Messenger observed at this the cunning of the man, and lapsed into silence. The boat had now swung round into the creek of the sea; and they began to row through a great gorge, which rose up, infinitely grand in the moonlight, to a height of at least three hundred feet above the beach. The steep and stony walls of this were half hid by the pines and clinging-plants which thrived generously upon it; yet there were stretches where the quartz-like ore gave a sheen as of burnished silver, and the lagoon itself shone like a mirror where the soft light fell. For the third part of a mile, at the least, the boat glided silently below the home of eagles and the wood-capped peaks, meeting no other craft; nor was there any sign of men until, with a sudden turn, the mouth of the tunnel came to their view, and a dozen rough fellows, gathered upon the small wall at the edge, hailed the boat's crew, and were answered with a hail again.

"Hola! que tal?" The cry was repeated thrice, and each time the echo of the sound boomed in the tunnel, and seemed to roll away to the very heart of the hills. At its second repetition the boat had come up to a great cave-like aperture; and, being rowed straight on, a weighty darkness closed the scene from the men's eyes; and they could distinguish only the glitter of rude lamps, which showed, in their limited aureola, walls green with slime, and water which shone black as the environing darkness. But, and this after the fashion of the creek without, the tunnel trended, when it had continued for some two hundred yards, sharply to the right; and, as the boat swung round on the bend, she came up to a small wooden platform in the wall, and there was held by a couple of seamen who carried lanterns in their hands, and appeared to be waiting for the party.

The exchange of greeting between the Spaniards was very brief. The man in authority at once stepped upon the platform and bade the Englishmen follow him through a wicket of iron set in the rock; and, when they had so done, they were in a narrow passage of brick, feebly lighted by oil lamps. The passage inclined upwards at a very sharp angle, and was so low that a stooping posture was necessary to those who walked in it; but the Spaniard set a quick pace up the incline, and presently they emerged upon a stone courtyard with exceeding high walls; and thence, passing another gate into a block of buildings, they continued through several corridors until at last they stood within the castle itself, as they surmised; and the guide bade them wait in the charge of three of the others who had accompanied him.

So far as Messenger could observe in the dim light, the building in which they now were had walls of immense thickness, and betrayed its age in every arch and pillar. Above them, a roof of stone sculptured with rich tracery, gave evidence of Moorish influence, and the slender columns which supported it

P

had much of the delicacy which is conspicuous at Granada. Yet the vast hall, or ante-room, or whatever it was, possessed scant ornament of furniture; though towering gates, emblazoned with shining brass, and many images with lamps burning before them, were a testimony to abiding care. The aspect of it, indeed, was one of sumptuous luxury, and led the imagination on quickly to depict gorgeous scenes behind the gates, whence came the murmur of fountains splashing and the low hum of voices.

In this hall the two prisoners—for Burke and the nigger were not brought there—waited for the space of ten minutes, standing moodily before their guides. At the end of that time one of the brass gates was opened, and the Spaniard returned, beckoning them to follow him. Nor did he appear to anticipate any attempt to escape, being alone with them after they had passed from the hall, and stopping a moment to cut the ropes which bound their hands. They were now in a lofty passage lit by lamps of bronze, and so thickly carpeted that the footfall was noiseless; a passage upon whose walls strange allegories, depicted with the brilliant colouring of the Spanish school, were lavished; and from the great corridor they passed to a circular and gilt-domed ante-chamber, where fountains bubbled up from the outstretched arms of nereids; and light fell cunningly upon marble basins and the sun-fish which swarmed in them. Never had they seen a chamber so perfect in its harmonious colouring, so seductive in its lounges, so suggestive of fine placidity of life; but hardly had they come into it when the the great Spaniard threw open curtains which hid one of the panels of its apse, and the pair of them stood in the presence of the Spanish woman.

The room was a lofty one, lighted by many candles set in a chandelier of Venetian glass; its panelled walls were decorated by sombre portraits. At its upper end an archway, hung with curtains, cut it off from a smaller apartment, which was just seen through open woodwork delicately carved; and there was a gallery running along one of its sides, with other doors leading into it. Yet was the most striking feature of the chamber the woman who sat in a low chair, surrounded by Great Danes, then snarling at the newcomers. As the light from a reading-lamp shone upon her face, the Spanish woman, whom Messenger had last seen for any certainty at Monaco, presented a countenance no less repulsive than upon the day of their first meeting. Her thick ropy black hair fell upon her shoulders in the fashion of the school-girl; her arms seemed as muscular as those of a strong man; her face was brown with the burn of the sun; her eyes shone with an unnatural lustre, and flashed light here and there as the eyes of an eagle. And as the two stood before her she searched them with her gaze so that they could scarce face her; and were conscious of a mysterious subtlety and power of which they had not known the like.

When the big Spaniard had withdrawn, the woman

spoke in English which had hardly a fault, but with a voice that grated on the ear like an unresolved discord.

"Well, Mr. Arnold Messenger," said she, "it is our privilege to meet again!"

At this, Messenger made the suspicion of a movement, but answered quickly—

"Madame, I do not remember that we have met before."

"No?" she said with emphasis, using a great fan of ostrich feathers cunningly. "Then you have lost your memory with your money—what a double misfortune!"

Now when she said this the man felt a twitch of every nerve in his body. That the woman knew his name was ill-chance enough; but that she made no disguise whatever of the other knowledge threw him so thoroughly off his mental balance that he answered her with a lie which was as clumsy as it was useless.

"Madame," said he, with a great simulation of regret, "my memory I may recover; but the money is now in the Atlantic, though by what means you heard of it I cannot conceive."

"By what means!" said she. "Indeed, you do little credit to your reputation. Here is your life and a description of your recent achievements in a dozen papers—Spanish, French, and English. They say that you are the most cunning——"

"It's very good of them," said Messenger lightly,

and feeling the ground more surely; "let us accept their opinion gratefully, and go on to speak of other things. I will begin by asking you a question: Why have you brought us here?"

"To have the pleasure of seeing the first rogue in Europe," she replied, with a slight laugh.

"Is your curiosity gratified?"

"Nay," said she, "you are not ill-looking, not by any means; and I think you must be clever. I am glad that you have come to no harm."

She said this with complete unconcern; but the man replied, with a shrug of his shoulders—

"I think it was well that I did not; there are others in Ferrol who have not yet the pleasure of your hospitality; they may return any moment, and will know exactly where to seek us."

"And the money?" she exclaimed with the same harsh laugh.

"The money is out in the sea," said Messenger doggedly.

"As the young man here will tell me, too, no doubt!" she continued, turning to Fisher, who had listened to the conversation with surprise at every word of it; and when she had looked at him with her sharp eyes she added—"A pretty boy; but not clever, I fear. These things should not be heard by one so young."

Upon this, she touched a bell at her side, and a Spanish servant, dressed in ceremonious black, instantly appeared.

"Conduct this gentleman to his room!" said she; and the man beckoned to Fisher, who followed him from the apartment without finding a word, since he was yet hoping that he would find in the place the one who alone interested him of all those he had seen in Spain. But when he was gone, the woman bade Messenger sit, and took up her words at once.

"Well," said she, "I am sorry not to find you clever. It was not worthy of you to lie so clumsily, seeing how little it serves you. A falsehood should be the last resort of genius. Had you not better tell me at once where the money is?"

"On what terms?" asked Messenger, with a slight betrayal of eagerness.

She leant back upon her seat and looked straight at him.

"Your life," said she, "and, as you will wish it, that of the boy."

Messenger could sit no longer.

"Madame," said he, standing before her, and holding back his passion with effort, "we are wasting our time. You must have the poorest opinion of me to propose that. I refuse, of course."

It was a critical moment, as he felt. Though ostensibly alone, he could see the savage eyes of men peering through the woodwork at the far end of the chamber; and even from holes in the face of a portrait quite near to him a man was glancing. Whether or no the next moment would bring death to him he did not know; but suddenly he played his only card

—though for one instant he had the idea of killing the woman as she sat, and trusting to the after-minutes for his opportunity. But she only looked at him with an infinite power of penetration; and her hand hovered upon the bell at her side.

"You are a bold man," said she presently. "I must really make up my mind about you."

"When you do that," said Messenger, "I counsel you to look all round. You cannot think that you and the nature of your profession are unknown to me, or that I have taken no precautions. My friend Jake Williams"—he remembered Kenner's story, luckily—"has already had some acquaintance with you in America. I expect him on the coast with fifty men every hour, and he will first seek me here."

She shrugged her shoulders, but her right hand still was dangerously near to the bell.

"Jake Williams, did you say?" she asked.

"No other," he answered.

"Ah!" said she, "then he is the man spoken of by the journals as Jake Kenner; and is he coming back?"

"Certainly," said he; "and, as he knows a little of your past, it might be troublesome if he missed us."

He said this slowly and impressively, as he hoped; but the woman, having heard his words, did not, to his surprise, give him any immediate answer.

In the silence which followed upon his speech, the deep breathing of the Spaniards was heard more clearly. He was perfectly aware of her thoughts as she sat, all drawn up in her chair, a black cape about her shoulders, her ravenous eyes seeing nothing but pictures which the mind gave her. He knew that she was weighing the measure of the risk which would follow upon his death; and was debating, at the same time, the possibility of finding the money without his aid. Had he been in her place, he would have taken the bolder course unhesitatingly, and no man from the *Semiramis* would have lived an hour; but he could not forget that she was a woman, and women have caution rather than boldness in any work to which they may set their hands. When, at last, she spoke, her words ran well with his surmises.

"Well," said she, taking up the point as though there had been no pause, " it was wise of you to send the American to Ferrol. He and I have scores to settle; but, *mon ami*, is it not probable that he is already on his way to England in the custody of the police?"

"Perfectly possible," replied Messenger, who grasped the point instantly, " but that will make no difference to us; he will have delivered our letters to others."

"And the others will cry abroad that you are on this coast with a million of money, or as much of it as you saved from the wreck, to protect you from me. What a clever idea!"

" It is not clever," said Messenger, shrugging his shoulders; " but it is our last card. If we sink, I am perfectly determined that you shall not have a shilling, unless——"

"Unless what?"

"Unless you help us. And I will make you this offer: I will pay you one-third of the whole sum got out of the wreck if you will put your men at our disposal for a week, and allow us in the meantime the shelter of this house. Pray think it out calmly. If we are out of the way, you may find the bullion; but the greater probability is that you will never find it. And if you should be so lucky, our friends, who will presently discover our absence, will immediately make the whole story public, with your share in it the loudest talked about. A moment's consideration should convince you that your whole interest lies with us."

At this she looked up at him, a smile withering upon her hard-drawn face.

"That's very well said," she cried, "but there are holes in your argument. Let me remind you that we may find what is missing before the sun rises. Do you think that we shall sit here idly and wait your pleasure? Indeed you don't, for you are not such a fool."

"I shall risk anything you may do," said Messenger; "it's the one risk I must take. Otherwise, I have rather the best case, and can afford to laugh at your efforts."

He had grown bolder as he felt her wavering and saw that she made no movement to touch the gong at her side. But the Spaniards were still pressing upon the grating, and at this last speech of his he could hear the murmuring of their whispering. As for the woman, his words turned her from her quieter mood to one of ostensible anger.

"I would not begin to laugh yet," she snapped; "there is time for that. I have done with you now; to-morrow I shall know my mind. But don't forget that I have offered you your life and that of the boy——"

"Or that I claim the lives of the others," said Messenger, in a burst of lofty generosity which fell in exactly with the part he was acting

"*You* claim?" she answered, her anger growing, "you claim! ha! I shall be compelled to teach you a lesson. As I live, you are the first man that has dared to argue with me in my own house——"

"Let us hope I shall not be the last," exclaimed Messenger, who saw that he had won the deal; "argument, madame, is the doorstep to reason."

"You are impertinent," she said, rising. "Next time we meet I shall take means to bring you to better behaviour."

When she had said this, she tapped twice upon the table with her fan; then she withdrew herself behind a panel which opened at the touch of her hand; and was gone from sight. She had flaunted away in a burst of anger, and her exit had been in some part melodramatic; but the man for whose benefit the performance was designed stood quite unmoved. He thought only that he had taken her measure, and found it rather shallow. For her threats he did not care a snap of the fingers; and, to his infinite satisfaction, he foresaw the moment when the end of the bargaining should restore to him all that yesterday seemed lost. With the woman's aid, he would reach South America in the face of all the British warships that floated; with her assistance he would put his heel on the schemes for his capture and grind them to shreds. A dream of success floated up from the thought and held him motionless. The first ambition which had prompted the great flight from London was potent again with all its aims and possibility. He could have hugged himself at the luck which sent him to such a shore and such a haven.

He was aroused from the contemplation of these visions by the sudden discovery that a servant stood at his side—a waiting-man, dressed sombrely in black, but with knee-breeches, and silver buckles upon his shoes. Whence the fellow had come he did not know; but he looked at the gratings, where he had seen the eyes of many men a few minutes before, and did not now behold a single face. The crowd of janissaries had vanished as a picture from a lantern-cloth; the room beyond was in utter darkness; only the one servant waited for him, and appeared to be impatient that he should go. Another man might have contemplated, under such circumstances, a quick dash for liberty; but he was too wise. Though he could not see them, he felt that many eyes watched him; that he had but to raise a hand, and he would be struck down as he stood.

Convinced of this, he followed the lackey from the room, and, passing to a narrow stone case, he mounted many flights of stairs, going upward, upward, until at last the man opened a heavy wooden door, which swung upon valves, and intimated to him that this was his apartment. As he stepped into the room, the door was locked behind him; but a cheery greeting reassured him, and he made the welcome discovery that he was caged with the others of his party, and that they had looked upon him as dead.

CHAPTER XXIII.

A WARNING IN THE FLESH.

THE first to speak was Burke.

" Hello, my dandelion!" said he; "so you've riz up, after all? Wal, you always were a shiner! How did you leave the she-devil in the black toggery? Did she ask particler after my health?"

"I'm sorry to say she forgot to mention you," replied the Prince; "she was too busy debating me. Where's the nigger?"

"Here, sah," cried Joe from a dark corner of the place; "quite flat, sah, or fall out of the window, sah; slap-up fine thing in windows, no trouble to open him; you go long way, heels up, sah, if you don't mind your eye!"

The light was very dim, but his meaning was plain, for the room in which the four had been shut was at the top of one of the towers of the castle, and the whole of its right-hand side was open to the air, there being a parapet not more than six inches high to prevent any man stepping from the prison and going straight down to the flags of the court a hundred feet below. Beyond this startling eccentricity of casement, the place had nothing uncommon, being built with thick stone walls and heavy beams above; but there was a table in the centre of it, upon which some bottles of common Spanish wine, together with a supper of meat and bread, were set; and the floor was strewn with rushes.

"Well," said Messenger, after he had looked all round, "this wouldn't be the place to give a small and early in, eh, Burke? Not quite the 'Metropole,' is it? What's the wine like?"

"Forked lightning coloured up with sulphur!" said Burke. "I took a sup jess now, not more than a quart; and it only wanted a bit of string to spin me!"

"And Hal," continued the Prince, turning to Fisher, who sat upon a bench looking with infinite disgust at the fatty meal upon the table, "you don't tell me how you fared."

"I didn't fare at all," said Fisher. "The man brought me up here and shut me in; that was the beginning and the end of it."

"I wish to Heaven it was the end of it!" cried the other. "Do you know what she wants, Burke? She asks for the whole of the cash in return for a free passage for the four of us. I call that modest!"

When Burke heard this he sat up wonderingly.

"All the stuff?" he asked.

"Every sovereign of it," said Messenger.

"I'd burn her old body to blazes before I'd give her ninepence!" said Burke. "What ken she do?"

"She may do many things. To begin with, she might poison us——"

"Blind me, I never thought of that when I swabbed up the vitriol! What did you say?"

"I said that I would give her one-third in return for her help."

"You did foolish! What is there ez'll prevent her banking the cash and then stretching you?"

"A little something which occurred to me before I made the offer. If she accepts my conditions, I shall send two of you to Ferrol to look for Konner; and, wanting him, to do his business."

"That's right along cute! Did it occur to you belike that there was a way out of this hole?"

"Just as much a way out as there would be from Newgate if the pair of us were there now."

"She came to know of the business from the papers, I'm supposing."

"Exactly. The mate of the *Admiral* was picked up, as I thought, and half the police in Europe are tracking us."

"Wal, I reckon I saw it from the first. You must have been blind to let the man go."

"If I'd have done anything else, the crew would have turned. It was the best thing possible."

"Maybe; but, if it was me ez had drawn a bead on him, he'd be among the martyrs now. Do you think the old girl will take the third?"

"I'll tell you better in the morning. I'm full of sleep now; and I'm going to take a drink of that sulphuric acid. This place is productive of thirst."

"Wal," said Burke, settling down at his length, "look out for fireworks; and if you're waking call me early——"

"If we're waking!" said the other with a momentary gloom. "It's just possible that we may not wake."

Fisher and the nigger had been asleep towards the end of the talk; and though the bed of rushes did not suggest the sweets of rest, the others, who had scarce closed their eyes during two days and nights, now endeavoured to imitate them. The fact that the room lacked a wall was in no way to be regretted in the heat of the early morning hours; and, for the matter of that, the spires and domes of the castle, shining below them in a flood of moonlight, gave rest to the eye and a picture of exceeding beauty. From the great arch which wanted glass they could look over the spread of the park away to the rippling sheen of the sea; and to the hill above the haven where their money lay. Nor was it to their comfort that they observed torches flaring here and there, like elf-fires upon the beach; and saw, on the more open swards of the downs, companies of men moving from place to place; and heard the shrill crying echoing from hill to hill as the signals were given or answered. Such a spectacle suggested many things—to Messenger, at any rate; and he, knowing the large probability that their haven would be discovered, saw in its discovery the corollary of his own death and that of those with him. For it was as certain as the rise of the moon that, once she had her hand upon the bullion, the Spanish woman would give no quarter, nor parley for a moment with the outcasts over whom chance had given her the mastery.

Such logical forebodings held the man from sleep for many hours. He sat watching the path of the torches, which appeared and disappeared like a Jack-o'-lantern. Oftentimes his heart quaked as he heard some unusually loud hail, and he said to himself, "They have found the creek." He was cold with a piercing chill at the mere sight of a lugger in the offing. But his fears, for that night at the least, were quieted in the middle watch when, of a sudden, the British warship, which had been cruising on the coast, anchored in the bay; and the lights upon the beach were instantly extinguished, while parties of Spaniards came running up to the great house and crowded into the courtyards. Then a deep stillness succeeded, and, believing that the danger was past, he drank again of the wine and lay upon the mattress of rushes, to sleep with profound languor for many hours.

When he awoke he found himself, to his unutterable surprise, in another room. He had observed the change as he opened his eyes and saw, in place of the bare stone and the rushes, a panelled ceiling of oak and the posts of a wooden bed upon which he lay. He was now in a room which had some stamp of civilisation—an arm-chair of leather, a table with books upon it, a glass above the chimney, and a timepiece set by his bed. He saw then that it was five o'clock, and, by the fall of the sun's rays and the heat, he knew that he had slept for twelve hours, and that the wine which he had taken had compelled him to utter oblivion. Indeed, he felt a great weariness in his limbs, a difficulty to set out events in order in his mind; and when he rose to his feet giddiness seized upon him, and he reeled into the chair. Do what he would, he could conjure no ordered picture of the yestereve; could bring his brain to no recollection of the absolute circumstances of the day he had passed through. Nothing but the ephemeral and flitting impressions of scenes and persons could he grasp; and for a long while he sat with the vacuous stare of the wandering.

The awakening from this state of mental coma was a violent one. He had walked round his room twice, taking scant observation of its contents, and then had turned to gaze upon the greensward of a small but highly walled court upon which his windows gave. He could look from his casement down upon the whole face of this enclosure, over whose grass high chestnut-trees cast a welcome shade; and suggested by the lazy rustling of their leaves that the atmosphere was not sleeping even under the sun's rays. At the first there was nothing in the grass court to interest him in any way, or to call his mind to coherence; but, at the second look, his blood seemed to freeze within him, and he caught at the

"THE BODY OF BURKE, THE SKIPPER, WAS HANGING FROM THE LOWEST BRANCH" (*p.* 259).

window for support. For the body of Burke the skipper was hanging from the lowest branch of the hither tree, and swayed upon the rope which held it, so that there was no doubt of the man's death, though his face was hidden by the foliage, and little but his legs could be seen.

The sight, as I have said, brought Messenger's mind instantly to its work. Under the shock the events of the night recurred to him quickly. He remembered every word he had spoken to the woman; he could narrate again his last conversation with the man whose body now hung from the tree; nice points of argument with himself were again before him. And of these, the first he discussed was the point which the hideous sight in the courtyard suggested to him. Why had the woman hanged Burke? There was only one suggestion possible. She had done it to frighten the three who lived. It was the lesson she was to teach him. But it had no such sequence for a man of his feeling, at any rate. Another would have thought, if but for a moment, tenderly of one who had worked with him, sharing possibilities and dangers, evil luck and good chance, hard board and free fare; but Messenger had no such thought. "There is one less to share," said he; and he flung himself in his chair again, but this time to think with unclouded mind.

The woman had not found the money; that was clear; and if the British cruiser were still in the offing, she had probably ceased to search for it. He asked himself, what if he could make terms, and trust to the after-days to make them better terms? She was only an adventuress, after all; once he were in possession of substance, it were ill-luck if he could not play the stronger hand. He did not forget, however, that any moment might take from him the power of barter at all. If she found the creek, then he would hang with Burke. He must act, therefore, on the inspiration if he would save his neck and Fisher's. It was curious that in all his scheming this thought of the lad came to him, yet come it did; and he knew that if he had seen the boy's body hanging where Burke's was, the sight would have been almost unbearable to him. But he seemed to feel that Fisher still lived; and, desiring to speak to the woman quickly, he beat upon the door, and, after continued knocking, it was opened, and the Spaniard stood before him.

Somewhat to his surprise, the man desired no intimation of his object. No sooner had he appeared than he nodded greeting to the prisoner, and at once led the way from the chamber. They passed together down a long corridor of stone, and thence seeming to come into the main building again, they continued on through a vast room whose oaken walls were hung with armour; and so through a suite of grand but faded apartments until they reached the hall of fountains and the room where the woman had sat at her first reception.

It was not in this room that Messenger was now

received, but in a smaller chamber behind the panel which had opened so mysteriously at the woman's touch on the previous evening. Here sat the crone perched up in a great arm-chair; but she was not alone. A ragged man, who carried a ragged cap in his hand, stood at her side, and was talking to her with a wealth of gesture which implied an exciting narrative. Nor did she betray any surprise that the Englishman had come suddenly to her; rather she welcomed him, and at once began to speak.

"I was about to send for you," said she. "There is news from the hills, and bad news, I fear; a company of carabineers left Vivero at dawn, and is now encamped five miles from here. There is an Englishman at the head of it, and as far as I can learn, this house is its destination."

At this news the man paled for the second time since he had left London.

"Are you quite sure of your information?" he asked.

"As sure as I can be from the words of this messenger. He thinks that another company has left Ferrol, and that the hills are full of men. We may expect a visit any time between now and midnight."

Messenger took a turn up the room, his hands plunged into his pockets, and his teeth pressing hard into his lips. For the moment his mind reeled as the danger seemed to enclose him, look where he would; but suddenly he stopped before the woman, and asked another question.

"Tell me," said he, "have you any way leading from this house which is not likely to be a high-road for troops?"

She laughed at the simplicity of the question.

"Do you think," she cried, "that I would live in any place where I could be taken like a rat in a trap?"

"I didn't suppose it for a moment," said he; "but that being so, I am going to tell you where the money is, and we will make the flight together."

"It is the only possible course," said she, answering him with like frankness; "there is trouble for both of us, though I cannot tell at present how far I am involved in it."

"I gather from your words," said he, "that this house is the immediate object of the attack. Could you hold out here while we got the money hid inland? They will scarcely force your doors if you refuse to admit them."

She laughed with a harsh note.

"*Mon ami,*" she cried, "you do not know the carabineers of Spain. If it is as I think, and my acquaintances in Madrid have been talking too loudly about me, these men have come here on a double purpose. The first part of it is to lay hands upon you; the second to do me a similar kindness. It is your presence upon the coast that has set the hornets loose. The Spanish Government has known about my work for ten years; it might have moved in another ten if the Englishmen in the city had not cried incessantly for action. For me, were you not here, the future would be simple; I should set out to-night or to-morrow for Vienna, and return here with the new year. After such a display of enthusiasm as this, they would leave me in peace for another generation."

"But now the case is different," he exclaimed, interrupting her; "there is a million of money in a creek off your foreshore, and it has to be got into the hills without a moment's delay. How far off did you say the troops were?"

"The man says three miles; but they have camped in the village for the night. Where their camp is, and who they are, I am now going to ride out and learn for myself. Luckily, the English ship weighed anchor and left an hour ago. I shall know the best and worst of it by nightfall. Before that, you and I can arrange in a word; the moment we put the hills between us and these men—for my proposition is that we strike for my other house near Finisterre after concealing ourselves until the troops have something to report—we divide what is to be divided, and take different roads——"

"It is a fair offer," said he, "and I accept it. But I must stipulate that you continue to give me the service of your men until my share is shipped at the first port possible."

"That was understood," she exclaimed as she rose; "we are losing minutes which may be wanted. You will now take the men necessary to bring the money here, while I am riding to Goozadoyro. By my return everything should be ready for us to leave at midnight. I sent my daughter to Carcubion this morning with three servants. There is nothing more I can command until you have done your work."

"I am sure of it," said he; "but I must ask for the assistance of my friends. I presume you have not served the others as you served Burke."

"I served him—*sapristi!* I had nothing to do with it. He struck down one of my servants in his room, and they killed him in a brawl. He was not clever, and I wonder that you regret him—you who are so clever!"

He muttered something in reply which was not audible, for his busy brain was asking the question, Was the woman cheating him with a fine tissue of lies, or was she honest? Though his intuitive faculty prompted him to hesitation, he drew from the one fact, that he was no longer a prisoner, the conclusion that the woman's policy towards him had completely changed; and when he followed her into the courtyard of the castle that conclusion became more powerful. Twenty men mounted on sturdy black ponies, and all armed with guns, waited for her, and greeted her appearance with loud shouts. That they had something to tell her was apparent, and when a burly man at the head of them had poured out a volley of protestation, she turned and said—

"They fear a night march, and that is what I fear. You have not a minute to lose. I shall not ride to the village yet, but when we have prepared everything we will go together. Here are your friends!"

"Can you trust the men," he asked, "in the work at the creek?"

"If I could not," said she, "it would bode ill for the venture, don't you think?"

Fisher and the negro had come out with her words, and stood seemingly amazed at their liberation; but it was no moment for history. While yet they greeted Messenger, the Spaniard whom the woman called Fernando, he who had been in authority on the night of the capture, brought two ponies into the courtyard, and began a hurried confabulation. At the end of it, the woman spoke again—

"I can think," she cried, "of no better plan than this: let the boy here and the man with him accompany the boats, while you ride with me to the heights. I can offer you no better security."

"I do not ask any," said he; "are you wise to waste time? Why should you not get the shelter of the hills at once?"

"Because," said she, with a slightly contemptuous laugh, "we may not be the only tenants of them; I prefer to see danger before I turn my back upon it."

"That's so," he replied. "I'm talking like a fool. Are the boats ready?"

She answered affirmatively; but he turned to Fisher and spoke quickly.

"Hal," said he, "go down with the man here and

show him the creek. Stand by him while he ships the money; and, whatever happens, don't take your eyes off it if he'll let you keep them on. You understand?"

Fisher nodded his head, being still full of his amazement, and turned to follow the Spaniard; but the other sprang upon the saddle of the pony, and rode out of the gate by the woman's side. It was a curious and, in some measure, ill-assorted cavalcade that now defiled over the greensward of the park. Twenty men, some with capes and some with jerkins, some with sombreros, some with the broad-brimmed hats of seamen, some with embroidered jackets of velvet, some with sheepskins, but all horsemen of consummate ability, hugged close to the side of the woman who led them, she sitting hunched upon the back of a thick-set grey cob. Slung upon their shoulders were the antique but picturesque muskets; long knives dangled at their belts; revolvers were in their holsters. Habitually given to chatter and to noise, they came out now in great silence, riding at a gentle canter through the park of the castle to the high plane of grass-land which gave them a view of the sea; and they stood upon the plateau to watch the coming of three boats from the haven of the tunnel to the creek wherein the survivors of the *Semiramis* had found refuge. At the end of an hour, they observed the boats to return; and, as the signal appointed was made by the leading craft, Messenger's heart leapt with the fever of his excitement.

Until this time it is to be doubted if the Spanish woman had believed the story which she had read in the English and other papers. She might have hoped that some money was brought from the wreck of the yacht to the shore; but that the vast treasure named was saved in any considerable part she could not believe. At this moment the whole knowledge of the truth appeared to come upon her; her face lighted up with a savage smile of joy; reaching out from her pony, she kissed Messenger upon either cheek, as is the fashion of the Spaniards.

"Oh, my friend," said she, "if I had known you ten years ago ——!" And with this vague intimation of pleasure, she suddenly cried out to the Spaniards; and, at her word, they spread abroad over the park; and, galloping with an irresistible dash and impetuosity, the whole party swept inland towards the distant woods and hills.

After the first wild sweep of freedom, the escort gradually reined in its horses, and drew back to an easy canter. Mounted men had left earlier in the direction of Vivero, and others were on the hill-tops, watching for a view of the troops; but, notwithstanding this, the party divided when it came to the woods at the edge of the first bay, which had been the Englishman's haven, and so was split up until but two men rode with Messenger and the woman. She, evidently, had planned to ride for the summit of the great promontory which the wrecked men had seen from the yacht; but she led the way with infinite caution, and her readiness and positive lack of all sense of danger stood out so unmistakably that the Prince seemed to lean upon her intellect as a child leans upon a strong man's.

A mile from the shore the path lay through a wood of pines, there being a mossy bed to deaden the sound of horses' tramping, and a luxurious canopy of leaves, through which the setting sun streamed redly. Here the woman reined in her pony and listened a moment.

"Do you hear any sound?" she asked.

"None," said Messenger, who had drawn rein with her.

"You have no ears," said she; "listen again, and tell me."

"Except for the bird whistling," said he, "I hear nothing."

She laughed at him.

"The bird whistling is my man Pedro!" said she. "We can go on—slowly."

The wood continued for a third of a mile or more, the path through it beginning to rise when they had gone a hundred yards, and thence mounting with a severe gradient—which the ponies attacked with the skill of habit—until it became but a ribbonway against a hill-side. After this, they entered a second wood, and, coming to the edge of it, they beheld, both upon the seaboard and inland, the country lying below them at a great depth; and the sea itself—still, with the glassy surface of a lake. But—and this only was of moment to them—in the hollow where the first village was, the sky-blue coats and red breeches of a company of lancers shone conspicuous in the clear light; and these men were leading out their horses, and presently, being mounted in haste, they galloped away quickly in the direction of the shore.

As the eyes of Messenger turned towards the sea, the explanation of this action was given to him. A coasting steamer, flying some flag which he could not read, was running very close in upon the foreland; and near, in pursuit of her, stood the British cruiser which had haunted the bay of the haven for so many days. From the high ground whence they looked down upon the scene, it was possible to observe both the danger of the flying ship and the commotion upon the shore which her appearance had brought about. Scores of wild men now flocked from the village to the sea; others, already standing upon the sandy beach, were waving their arms and running hither and thither, as though they could help the one ship on or arrest the pursuit of the other; the lancers themselves were riding along the low land, and appeared to be waiting for the cruiser to drive the crew of the steamer ashore. The latter vessel was now forced in so close upon the land that the probability of her striking the rocks of the promontory was apparent even to Messenger; but before he could give words to his thoughts the woman at his side spoke them for him.

"*Voyez-vous, mon ami,*" said she, "here is news."

"I was thinking so," he answered. "I wonder if Kenner is aboard her?"

"We shall know soon," she cried. "Look at that!"

The exclamation followed a crash of shot from the pursuing vessel; and, as the shell fell into the sea before the steamer's bows, she dropped anchor and lowered her flag. At the same moment, a boat was put off from her side, and three men entered it—the foremost being Kenner. He had hoped to reach the shore before the long-boat, now let go by the other, could come up with him; but as his men bent their backs to the work, the woman cried, and this time with feeling.

"Look!" she said; "my score against your friend is about to be paid. If he puts ashore on those sands, Heaven help him!"

"He cannot escape the mounted men, anyway," said Messenger; "well, he was always a tenderfoot. I looked for him to come five days ago."

He spoke callously, though he felt much, and truly Kenner's position was critical. The cruiser's boat was coming in towards the shore at a great pace; his own men were struggling with the current, which swept their dinghy towards the neck of the peninsula. Their first intention of landing, and doubtlessly of making a dash for the hills, was checked when they perceived the troop of cavalry now standing prominent upon the beach; and while they hesitated the seamen of the cruiser drew up to them with long and powerful strokes.

Thus the position stood when Kenner—no longer able to tolerate the suspense—leaped boldly from his dinghy to the sea, and began to swim towards the sands. A great cry from the shoremen followed his venture; and, as he came in the shallows where he could walk, the cry was taken up again, as a cry of warning.

"Wait for it now," said the Spanish woman, "he is on the death-patch, and the lancers have had their ride for nothing."

The scene was exciting almost beyond endurance, even viewed from the distant height of the hill as they viewed it.

There, upon the sand, the water lapping about his knees, Kenner swayed and hesitated, while the men of the beach bellowed their warnings, and the pursuing boat drew so near that a seaman at the bows rose to clutch the hunted man. Driven by a hundred impulses and fears, the American at last made two or three quick steps in the endeavour to throw himself flat upon the water; but he tripped in the effort, and reeled so that he dropped at last upon his knees, and was engulfed to his waist. In that supreme moment his pitiful cry rose up from the water, and echoed from hill to hill, the death-cry of a man who feared death alone. It was pitiful to look upon his struggles as, inch by inch, the sand gripped him, and he saw himself going down to the oozing grave at his feet.

And the irony of it was that none could give him help, not even the men of the ship's boat who had come to arrest him—for the place wherein he sank had not a foot of water over it, and the boat grounded upon its edge, leaving the seamen to watch his doom. Thus, with one long piercing scream, he went down; and as the waters closed above his head, the spell of the grim scene was broken, and the men upon the beach, who had been held nerveless, began to move again. The lancers returned towards the village; the Spanish woman whipped up her pony and began to descend from their place of watching.

"It was a strange meeting," said she, "that of your friend and myself; but life is full of these things. We must think of ourselves now. Let us haste, for dark is coming down."

CHAPTER XXIV.

BEACONS ON THE HEIGHTS.

THE woman rode for some way in silence and with great caution in the precipitous descent. She did not seem to fear any immediate press of danger from the neighbourship of the troops, and when Messenger asked her, she answered curtly—

"We have the best of them by an hour, and that is enough. They have something to report now, and may sleep on it." After that she left it to her pony to feel his way down the hill-side, and did not even press him to the canter when they entered the woods again.

She had said that night was coming down upon them; but as yet there was only a shimmer of twilight seen through the canopy of branches, though the breeze sang with a melancholy note in the heights of the pines, and the grass rustled with the uneasiness it betrays often at sunset. Otherwise the woods were very still; no living soul seemed to tread them; the multitudinous birds were roosting; the herds of hogs were lying lazily upon the sward; even the streams trickled lazily as burns wearying for rest. At any other time the scene would have glowed with an infinite charm for all who enjoyed it; but the two who now beheld it were harassed by so many thoughts, so many hopes, even by so many fears, that its beauties escaped them. They only rode on in mutual silence—glad of the solitude and of its meaning.

They must have now come within a mile and a half of the castle, and had reached an open clearing where they had some view of the wood-capped heights of their own bay. Here the woman drew rein for the first time on the homeward journey, and looked up expectantly to the highest of the peaks which towered above her home. A thin, cloud-like reek of smoke was rising up from it; and, as they stood to observe it, the cloud broke into bright flame, such as would exude from kindled logs. This beacon, rapidly becoming a bush of light, was quickly answered by the flare of a second fire on the nearer hill; and soon, from peak to peak and valley to valley, the signal flashed—woods lighting up as fairy scenes where the glow spread upon them; the granite rocks all ruddy as ore of ruby where they stood incarnadined; the chasms of quartz and marble and granite glowing with a sheen of a thousand lights in the play of the flames which shot up from crags and ridges, from the swards of the forests, and the open faces of the woodland glades.

The desolate land had, indeed, become alive with the life of its beacons. Though no man was seen upon the hills, though the silence of nightfall yet lingered in the woods, Messenger felt that many watched near to him, that unseen hands were working to the safety of the woman, and thus to his own security. He scarce hazarded the question, "Of what moment is the signal?" as he rested upon the pony's back and watched the path of the fire. But she, when she had remained motionless for many minutes, of a sudden set spurs to her beast, and, as the man laboured after her, she gave him the explanation.

"They have lit the fires—there is danger in the hills, then. *Du courage, mon ami!* It will be a clever fellow who shall lay hands upon me in my own house. But ride, ride!—ride as I ride!"

She set the good example with her words, and never man rode as she rode. Messenger had a fine knowledge of horsemanship, but scarce could he keep with her as she dashed, by thicket and bramble and through the darkening groves, onwards to the flickering lights which now marked the work of her own men in the park of the Castle. Nor was her mad flight a mere freak of excitement, as the man at one time thought; for, scarce were they come to the last thicket which lay between them and the open sward, when five mounted carabineers, whose dark-blue coats looked black in the failing light, forced their horses upon their path, and called loudly for them to stop. So sudden was their appearance that the woman had hardly drawn rein and pulled her pony upon its haunches, when both she and Messenger were among the company, and their leader rode forward to lay his hands upon the Englishman. But at this the hag rose upon her stirrups like a fury, and, striking the man across the face with the butt-end of her whip, she felled him to the ground at the blow.

As the man fell, his four companions stood back dumb before the fury of the crone. But she, cursing them fiercely in Spanish, drew two pistols from her holsters with amazing readiness. One she gave to Messenger, and, with the other in her bridle-hand, she cackled—

"Follow where I lead, and shoot when I shoot. I count upon you."

The readiness of the woman was as remarkable in this vital moment as it had been all along. While she yet spake the words, she wheeled her pony round and galloped back for twenty yards; but there she wheeled again, and set spurs to the brute so that it bounded forward with the agony; while the man imitated her, and, driving his horse forward headlong, he rode at the four. So irresistible was the charge that the carabineers instinctively held back in their saddles as the witch neared them—a horrid figure of a woman screeching with uncontrollable rage—and she, as she swung outward from her pommel, fired twice at their horses; and the brutes reared and plunged before her, and galloped madly into the woods. Of the others, Messenger shot one in the forehead, whereon the man's horse raced away with him, dragging a corpse at the saddle; but the fourth, in no wise fear-stricken, let the pair pass him, and then loosed rein for the pursuit.

The vigour and courage of the charge had now carried the pursued into the open park, where the veldt was smooth as a green, and the ponies flew on with the mad gallop of fear. The carabineer at their heels had pulled a pistol from his holster, but had no skill at shooting from the saddle, and his bullets skimmed the ground or whistled high in the air, or were buried in the turf immediately before him. Yet still he held on, and, shouting loudly with the intense heat of chase, he was presently answered in loud whoops from the woods by the sea, whence came a company of lancers at the gallop. They were the men from Vivero, and it was evident that they had seen the woman as she rode, and were set to the pursuit of her. But at the sight of them she laughed again with her wild harsh laugh, and her pony, as if in sympathy, bounded forward in the momentous race.

The two, as I have said, were now upon the fine stretch of lawn-like land which ran up to the moat on that side of the castle where the keep was. Inspired by the proximity of stables, and by knowledge of the environment, the ponies here gathered themselves together, as rabbits that press upon a warren; and snorted with the freshness of their pace and their own pleasure at it. Yet, with all their efforts, they would scarce have outpaced the troopers, had not the shoremen come to their aid, and at the very moment when that aid was needed sorely. Scarce, indeed, were the riders in the home park when a great crying went up from the purlieus of the mansion; wild arrieros and hillmen came crowding upon the wooden bridge which stood across the moat for lack of drawbridge; they roared encouragement to the pursued and oaths upon the pursuers. Then running, some for their muskets and some for their pistols, they threw themselves flat upon the grass, and began to pick off the galloping cavalry with a skill which could be looked for only among nomads of the hills.

At this sight the Spanish woman cut her pony fiercely with the whip, and took new heart. She had been riding for some time crouched down upon her brute's neck, fearing the pistol bullets of the carabineers; but when her own men began to shoot she sat upright again, and gave her approval with a reckless flow of curses and encouragements which must have been heard away upon the sea. And in her exulting joy she circled about Messenger, so speedy beyond his was her pony, and shared with him her anticipations.

"Once beyond the bridge, *mon ami*, there is safety—safety! Let them follow me then! I have a hundred men at the gates, and another hundred upon the hills. Let them come if they care nothing for their lives. Holy Virgin, what music!"

It was the music of musketry that she spoke of—the music of a rattling volley fired by the mercenaries upon the grass-land. And so well did they shoot that twenty of the horsemen reeled back in their saddles with the echo of the report; and twenty more at the least fell headlong upon the turf with dead or dying brutes beneath them. Then for the first time the troopers checked their pace, and, swerving right and left from the deadly attack, they reined in for consultation. But this was the woman's opportunity. As a second volley flashed upon the failing light, she rode furiously across the gravel pathway which led to the bridge; and, Messenger being at her heels, they presently drew up amongst their men with a great clatter of stones and ponies reeking; and were welcomed with guttural shouts that rang through court and cloister as the cry of a victorious army.

CHAPTER XXV.

THE SECOND PERIL OF THE CREEK.

IN the first unrestrained reaction of success, the pandemonium that arose in the inner quadrangle of the castle was beyond words. Muleteers, serving-men, shepherds, masters of coasters, hillmen babbled and gesticulated with a vigour which defied all the woman's demand for silence. Of the vast throng not a half were armed with guns or pistols; but the swarthy majority flourished shillalahs or plain clubs, or the shining cuchillos, and seemed bent upon an immediate sortie to the destruction of the cavalry or of anything or anybody that they might hap upon. And now they swarmed about Messenger and the woman, whose reeking ponies were half hid in a cloud of steam, and demanded orders, or suggested them, or reeled off oaths, or uttered shrill "*olés*" with all the awakened spirit of the rarely awakened Spaniard.

Such a scene might have been prolonged even to the morning had it not been for the near presence of the pursuing cavalry in the park. Even above the clamour of the horde, and while the woman was commanding silence in vain, there came the sharp sound of shooting, coupled with the duller reports of the old smooth-bore guns with which many of the Spaniards were armed. And again after that, while a semblance of a hush had fallen upon the company, there were those that came into the quadrangle, carrying dead or dying, and calling out that the troopers had begun to shoot, and were advancing rapidly to the very gardens of the mansion. Then only was the woman heard, and as she gave her orders her voice rang out with the penetration of a bugle-note.

"Call them in," she cried in Spanish, "call them in, and stand by the bridge. At the shot of the pistol, let the chains go! Fernando, is all ready below?—then take your place here, and hold the gate as you would hold your lives."

They had blown a horn almost with her order; and at that signal the mob without ran in quickly over the bridge, and came raging into the courtyard; some showing wounds, others telling of men shot and of escapes. But the lancers mounted again, and came swiftly over the turf towards the suspended bridge, a young officer leading them with drawn sword.

"Now," said the woman, as she watched their advance with a grim smile upon her blackened features, "now—let them swim!" and with that she fired her revolver at the boy leader when his horse had actually set foot upon the boards, and, as he fell forward, she gave a fiendish cry, and, the chains being let go, horse and man fell crashing into the moat. A dozen troopers, unable to check their advance, rolled over upon them, so that presently horses and men surged together in the water; and the screams of anger and of pain rose up from the ditch. In the same moment the great gates of the castle clanged upon their hinges, and shouts of defiance again echoed in the courtyard.

The shutting of the gate closed the first scene of the strange contest. The soldiers in the park had no artillery with them, and it is to be doubted if they would have used them had there been a dozen batteries. They had come across from Vivero, looking for nothing but the capture of certain Englishmen said to be upon the coast; and the woman was misinformed in the particulars of their wish to arrest her. They had no such wish or instruction; but had been drawn suddenly into this serious brawl whereby they had lost forty of their men; and now there was no one armed with a sufficient measure of authority to know what steps to take; and they remained aimlessly riding before the gates, and waiting for those who should come up from Ferrol. That help, and a force large enough to make poor work of the Countess Yvena's resistance, was within a mile of them, they knew; and, although they had a certain hope from the presence of a Spanish gunboat which now fired a signal gun in the bay, they had perforce to remain idle while the mob within the gates mocked them, and even fired shots from the bastions.

To this delay, and the wide dispersement of the

"'NOW—LET THEM SWIM!'" (p. 281).

troops in the valleys about the great house, the Spanish woman and Messenger owed their immediate safety. As the mob of serfs swarmed into the great quadrangle, the woman entered the hall of fountains by a wicket from the cloisters of the quadrangle, and stopped to drink a prodigious draught of water. The Englishman dipped his face in the marble basin, and tried to concentrate his mind upon the danger which stood all about him—in the hills, in the valleys, in the company, even upon the sea. Kenner had come, truly—but to what an end! The woman had promised him safety; but what were her words worth? He lived; but how soon would the law put a hand upon him? Only the one thought—the money, writ large as in golden letters—maintained him in that feverish excitement and unrest upon which he lived then, and which tightened his nerves so that they twitched as the nerves of an epileptic.

From such reckonings with gloom and possibility the voice of the woman recalled him.

"This is no hour to loiter," said she, "and they wait for us. Everything goes as I hoped. We shall be miles in the hills before sunset, and by to-morrow night these troops will return to report my house empty. Did I not tell you that I would never be taken here? Well, they have an equal task before them in the mountains! Come, *mon ami*, we will sup yet in the woods above Mondonedo!"

"They have brought the kegs from the creek,

then?" he asked, as he brushed his wet hair from his forehead.

"Every one of them," she replied, "and they are now loading the mules. I do not grudge you your triumph, *mon cher*. I did not believe, could not—you understand?"

"Perfectly; I doubt if I believe it myself, even now. But I am ready."

As she talked, she had poured out two glasses of strong liquor, and, putting a cigar-box before him, she offered him a light, while she rolled herself a cigarette with incredible rapidity. Then she strode from the apartment, and he followed her through the gate by which he had first reached her house. In the smaller outer courtyard two men, who carried lanterns, waited at the iron door of the inclined passage which led to the tunnel in the creek; and, immediately entering by the narrow archway, they shut out the sound of voices as they locked the wicket, and quickly descended to the cavernous depths below.

Once in the tunnel, a vast silence reigned. Two sentinels—rough Spaniards, whose hair flowed over their shoulders, and whose curious apron-like dresses were covered with many beads of coral and of silver—stood at the seaward entrance, armed with rifles. The flicker of a few torches cast an amber light upon rough, bearded seamen, who lay with their guns in postures of defence upon the edge of the narrow quay. It was along this quay that the woman, lighted by a single torch-bearer, now went with a ready step; and, coming out of the cavern at length upon the landward side, showed the inner and final lagoon, which stood as a tiny natural harbour in the very depths of her own grounds.

Here, as Messenger soon observed, was the haven of her seclusion. High walls of rock edged about the lagoon on every side; trees grew thickly upon the cliffs of it; there were innumerable small warehouses of stone built at varying heights above it; and, on the southern side, a steep path, cut through the rock, ages gone, by some falling rivulet, was now hewn out into a hill road, upon which a drove of mules, whose bells lacked their clappers, had been tethered.

In this place the woman hid what plunder the wolves brought her from the sea: and here, now, the two black boats were moored, while a dozen sturdy arrieros, armed to the teeth, dragged the kegs from them and bound them to the backs of the mules. And here Fisher and the negro worked by torchlight like navvies, transmitting their energy to the others, who hauled and pulled, and muttered oaths almost with every action.

At the coming of the party, which was quickly put across the pool in a punt waiting for it, Fisher sprang up and greeted Messenger warmly.

"I'm glad you're here," said he; "it's been a dreadful time! There's a boat from the Spanish ship cruising in the bay, and we expect her every minute.

We shan't have all the stuff loaded for another half-hour yet!"

"Is it all there?" asked the Prince, who jerked out his words with significant emphasis.

"Every ounce of it; and we had luck with us. The Spanish ship anchored ten minutes after we had come into the cove. What I want to know now is, How are you going to get the two large cases on a mule's back? You might as well ask him to trot off with a cathedral!"

"We'll see to that; get the rest loaded. I must speak to her about it. Hal, it's a crushing business!"

"Old man, that's true! I seem to be living with my head on fire. Heaven knows where we'll all be to-morrow!"

"Out of this, anyway; but I see that she's bringing barrels up. She's quick, isn't she? She must have seen the big case as we crossed. I never knew a woman with such a head!"

"Nor I," said Fisher, who had an eye for the beautiful.

The woman, as they saw, had anticipated their difficulty. At her direction the great case of sovereigns was broken open, and as the Spaniards stood a moment dazzled by the brightness of the gold under the torches' light, she, too, raised her hands dramatically; and then, with a stamp of her foot, recalled them to their work. They obeyed her with renewed efforts; but the sovereigns were still being heaped into the smaller barrels, when there was a low whistle from the tunnel, and all the workers doused their torches in the water as by a common impulse.

"What is it?" asked Messenger, as he, with the others, lay flat upon the quay and listened. He was answered by a rippling of the water in the pool, and a distant sound of oars. He waited, breathing with an effort, and the sound became more distinct—the boat was coming up the creek to the tunnel, and the Spaniards were whispering among themselves. Then the woman, putting her hand upon his as he drew a pistol, spoke.

"Hold that back, if you don't want a hundred men in here," said she; "it's a Government boat from the bay, and they are making their last voyage."

The boat was now very near to the tunnel's mouth, yet so perfect was the silence of the Spaniards, who had withdrawn into the inner lagoon, that the creek might have been the home of desolation rather than of men. Not a sound, scarce a breath, was heard; but the sailors in the boat began to discuss the situation, and presently lit a blue-flare in the tunnel; though even then the bend of it prevented them seeing the garrison, which was now waiting with high-strung eagerness. Yet by what means his friends were going to cope with the danger, or to overcome it, Messenger could not tell. Not a man of the defending party had a gun raised; not one drew a knife; they only lay crouching upon the rock, with expectant grins upon their swarthy faces, and their heads down almost at a level with the water.

Was the boat coming on or going back? The question was vital to them, the pause exasperating. Their nerves were now so knit-up that they moved restlessly in spite of themselves, and the deep gasps of men trying to hush their breathing were distinctly to be heard. They knew well that if they permitted escape to the attackers, they might as well give themselves over to the soldiers at once. And they could hear the bated discussions, the low talk, the arguments of those who unwittingly stood so near to death; and still the boat did not advance, while the flare died down, and darkness reigned again. Then, suddenly, the whole of the watchers gave a simultaneous movement of unrest, and crouched as beasts that await their prey. The boat was rippling onward; was being punted, in the light of a lantern, through the tunnel; and, as the water from its prow lapped the stonework, the Spaniards prepared quickly for action.

It was at this moment that the woman's design first became apparent to Messenger. He saw, as some of the Spaniards crawled swiftly into the cavern, what he had not seen before. A great portcullis of iron covered the shoreward end of the tunnel—which here had comparatively a small arch—and this portcullis was now to do the work which neither knife nor pistol could do. It was at the best a rough contrivance, drawn up with chains which turned about iron drums; but the spikes at the lower end of it were heavy as pike-heads, and the weight of it was to be measured in tons. Towards such a trap the long-boat now came slowly; and the party watched as they would have watched a snake waiting to strike a rabbit.

At the very head of the tunnel, less than a half of the boat being in the lagoon, the rowers ceased to work, and stood under the death-trap while they lighted another flare. As the brilliant blue-light flashed up, and the whole of the Spaniards instantly became visible, the sixteen seamen in the craft uttered a loud shout of triumph, and sprang to their oars again; but it was their last action. In that instant the Spanish woman, with hands clenched and streaming hair, cried out in a shrill treble voice, which rang through the cave, and the great portcullis, being let go at the drums, fell, with a grating of iron and a horrid crash, upon the boat and its crew; and the shout of triumph became a shout of agony.

The fall of the iron gate split the long-boat as a hammer will split a nut. One of the lance-like bars drove right through the body of a burly seaman sitting amidships, and, cleaving his skull, ultimately pinned him upon the bottom of the pool as a moth is pinned upon a board. The craft herself was shivered and crushed down upon the hard rocks, and, being cut almost in half, the two ends of her rose up all splintered, and were gripped furiously by the seamen, now at their last extremity. Of these, four were

S

held down under the sluice of the tunnel, but two rose on the seaward side of the portcullis, and ten in the pool; and all of them, swimming or clutching wreckage, or seeking to come to the quay, cried out for mercy most pitifully.

As well might they have clamoured for the fall of the sky. Urged on by the Spanish woman, who shouted incessantly, the defenders began to use their clubs and knives with savage jubilation. Where a face showed above the water they struck at it; they beat and cut the hands of the driven men who held to the quay; they dived boldly into the water and stabbed those who had harbourage at the fragments of the broken boat. In ten minutes there was not a cry; not a sound where there had been uproar. Only a breathless throng of savage men, whose clothes were in many cases dripping upon their backs, whose hands were weary with the pursuit of the butchery.

Thus was the peril from the sea turned; and at the end of another hour, it being then near to eleven o'clock, the whole of the money had been bound to the backs of the mules; and the party moved up the steep road from the creek, and soon gained the wooded heights at the back of the castle.

CHAPTER XXVI.

A STRANGE CRY IN THE HILLS.

THE night was clear, with a fine flood of moonlight, and after the first ascent to the heights the path became narrow, running through a great ravine of the mountains, which so sheltered it that its security from all but the hillmen was unquestionable. It was, in truth, a path which Nature might have cut for the peculiar protection of those in the great house below; and, while Messenger wondered at first that the soldiers knew nothing of it, he had no surprise when ultimately he had traced it to its end.

The cavalcade which now mounted this hidden way was by no means an unpicturesque one. At the head of it there walked six men with guns upon their shoulders; men dressed in the finery of velvet and silver-broidered habiliments. Behind them came sixteen mules, lacking the customary bells, but bedecked with fine ribbons and rosettes, as are all the mules of Spain. The arrieros, or muleteers, sat in many cases upon the top of the kegs and packages which the mules bore; but others walked, cracking their whips at the difficult places, and muttering the "*macho, macho, macho-o,*" which is the national encouragement to horse or ass. In the rear of the mules the Spanish woman, Messenger, and Fisher rode upon ponies; while six more personal attendants, armed with rifles, followed them. The nigger Joe whipped in the whole, sitting upon a sturdy "burro," like a sable Sancho upon a Spanish ass.

For a mile, or even more, the curious procession marched in silence; but when it had gained the first woods, which stood between two of the nearer mountains, the woman reined in her pony, and surveyed the scene spread out below her. Straight down, as it were at her feet, she could look in the courtyard of her home, where there were now many lanterns, and soldiers tethering horses, and the flash of polished helmets. Out upon the sea the masthead lights of the two warships burned brightly; in the park the flare of fires showed the new camps of the shoremen. But the whole spectacle excited the woman to merriment rather than to concern.

"Let them do their worst!" said she mockingly. "I will return before the year has run, and reckon with them."

"If they don't reckon with you first," said Messenger.

"Pshaw!" she cried, "it will be the affair of the month. I have friends at Madrid who will think of me—and ministries, *mon ami*, ministries fall. Let us get on while dark holds, for day must find us many miles from here."

"I hope it will," said the man; "the stake is big, and is worth the danger."

"Danger! You talk always of danger. There is no more danger now—I tell you so, and I am no optimist. Let us go."

She gave rein to her pony, and the man turned with her; but while she hurried to join her company there came from the heights above them a weird wild cry, which echoed in all the hills, and died away with a long-drawn sob, most pitiful to hear.

So mournful was it, so long did its vibration ring in the heights, that the whole of the riders stopped abruptly, waiting to hear its repetition; but although they halted for many minutes, the cry was not raised again; nor was there any sound save of the restless sway of the pines and the tremble of the grasses. To the Spaniards the very silence was ominous, the portent of ghostly visitation or of mountain spirit. They knew that they had little to fear from any human enemy in the almost inaccessible pass; but their faith was chiefly in omens, and they began to beat their breasts or to recite their rosaries, while one or two fell upon their knees and did not hide their panic. Even the woman herself was for a moment bewildered, and could find no words, only looking at Messenger inquiringly.

"What, in Heaven's name, was that?" she asked him presently. "Was it the cry of a beast? It ran down my spine like cold water!"

"I should say that it was the shout of some hillman gone out of his wits at the sight of the fires," said he; but he only told her half the truth, for he was sure that he had heard the cry before, although he could not now recall the precise circumstances.

"I've lived here half my life," said she, "and never heard its like. It was no human cry, or the men would make light of it. Look at them now!"

The spectacle was unmistakably odd, for the cut-throats, who had devoted the previous hour to the gratification of their savage lust for murder, now prayed with the feverish piety of the fanatic; and the simpler muleteers stood grovelling with their fears.

"When they have quite finished their exercise," said Messenger, as he watched them contemptuously, for he had begun to recover himself, "they might as well get on, unless they wish for the company of the men below. At this rate, morning will trap us in the woods here!"

"You are quite right," said she. "But you must admit that it was strange. I have never heard anything so wild."

The woman's superstition had undoubtedly done for her what human danger could not have done. For the first time since the Englishman had known her, she had lost her readiness; and when, at last, she began to shout at her servants, it was with but a half of her earlier vigour. Nor did she, after this, give any immediate sign that she had forgotten the episode, for she rode a long way in silence; while the others, equally dumb, followed her thoughtfully. To Messenger, the cry had been the echoing of some voice of the unremembered past; to Fisher, it was a cry which seemed to utter a warning that the end of the hazardous venture was near, though for this he had no reason save the shallow faith which every man in his own way gives to omen.

The strange company had now reached the summit of the pass, and traversed a dark road through an exceedingly close wood, on either side of which bold, treeless rocks, with insurmountable precipices, made a natural fortress. The one danger of pursuit lay, so far as Messenger could see, in the possibility of the troopers bursting the portcullis of the lagoon; and as he went on, and the pace of the mules seemed every minute to be more exasperating, he found himself listening for the tramp of infantry or the whinnying of horses.

"You seem to make the poorest way," said he to the woman at last. "What if they come up here from the house? we are no better then than rats in a trap."

"If they come up!" she cried, with her grim laugh; "if they cut through six-inch iron bars and two doors of steel in twenty minutes—let them!"

"But they will certainly find the road before daylight—and then?"

"*Mon ami*, let me answer you in the old proverb: 'He who despises a woman's counsel is a fool!' Do you judge of me so poorly as to believe that I have not thought of that?"

"I merely point out what occurs to me; but I will take your word for it. I must say the same of the road ahead of us. Suppose that is closed by troops——"

She laughed again unrestrainedly.

"Wait until you have passed it," said she, "and you shall tell me then what sort of a road for troops you find it; but we are near the bridge, and I am going to show you why no one shall follow me here."

As she spoke they had emerged from the wood, and stood upon the edge of an immense ravine, which seemed utterly to block egress from the amphitheatre. Long grass and weeds grew upon the bank of the precipice, down which the man of weakened nerve might scarce trust himself to look. The pines were thick even to the border of the chasm. But the muleteers, turning their beasts dexterously upon the brink of the abyss, marched for more than a quarter of a mile at the very side of it, and then came suddenly upon a small drawbridge of iron suspended upon chains from the far side.

Across this bridge the cavalcade went quickly at the woman's orders; but the last of the serving-men, when they had made the transit, worked briskly at a rude windlass, and drew the structure up perpendicular against their own side of the ravine. The whole danger of the pursuit was thus cut off, so far as the rear of the little expedition went; and from that time the spirits of the Spaniards rose, and they began even to hum their ballads and to smoke the indispensable cigarrito. The way had become an ideal one. Luxurious grass was beneath their feet; the strong scent of rich flowers and of hay came up to them upon the refreshing breeze; the hills around shone like domes and spires of marble in the glorious moonlight. Above all, they had put the first barrier between themselves and their enemies; and the road to freedom seemed open.

"Well," said Messenger, as he urged his pony to the trot, and rode on with the woman, who now put herself at the head of the company, "I admit that I was wrong. The place seems honeycombed with paths. If all the road is like this, we should reach Finisterre. I wish I could be as sanguine as you are."

"Hope, my friend," said she in answer, "is the keynote of enterprise. I told you that our real dangers will begin when we leave the mountains; but I think they are to be met. Directly we are in the open we shall break up, and make for my châlet in twos and threes. If any are taken, well, that will be a misfortune; but it must be faced."

"How far will the troops follow us?"

"They—they will return to their quarters at the first opportunity. A Spanish carabineer does not follow anyone. He is the guardian of law and order —when it come in his way; otherwise, he assumes that all is well with the world. Of course, this is a more serious case, for men have been killed. But we forget an *émeute* very quickly in Spain, especially if we have friends; and I have many."

"And once at Finisterre?"

"We shall get a ship and sail for the Adriatic, and after that for the East, if you will listen to me. All you Englishmen run for shelter to America; it is your mistake. I have a haven near Scutari where no Government could find me. We will share it until this is forgotten; then, perhaps, we will return here."

He shrugged his shoulders, for the prospect was not to his liking; but this he did not tell her, since they were now beginning to skirt a low hill, upon which one of the beacon-fires still burned.

The deep red light cast a lurid glow upon the pine forests beneath. When the men turned at length and entered a wooded ravine, which led from the amphitheatre between the heights to the outer country, the flicker of it was strong, lighting even the tangled depths of the forest path. By the light of such a rude lantern, they emerged from the valley, to come upon a narrow ledge running around the outer side of the hill, and this being no more than three feet wide, with woods upon the left hand and a deep precipice upon the right, the march was slow, and not a little hazardous.

Below this ledge of rock a long and fertile valley, dotted with hamlets and pastures, spread for many miles. Even by the moon's light, the land had a fair aspect; the breeze upon the heights was exhilarating as strong wine. The Spaniards, trusting in the sure steps of the mules, did not even come down from their saddles; the woman set a brisk pace, gossiping to Messenger behind her with the flippancy of a girl of twenty. Nor did a remote possibility of peril appear to threaten them, when the first signal of their ultimate hazard rose up on the night air.

It was the repetition of the wild weird cry they had heard in the first of the woods.

Suddenly, with the piercing wail and long-drawn sob, the cry rose in the forest above the goat-track. Once, twice, thrice they heard it, with stiffening of limbs and hearts palpitating. Then it was echoed back from the depths below them in the cry of a strong man hailing a friend.

"Halloa," said the invisible voice, "halloa-oa-oa! Billy, where are you? Show yourself, Billy!"

If one risen from the dead had confronted Messenger, he could not have been struck with a greater fear than he knew in that moment; for the second voice he recognised as the voice of Mike Brennan, the drunken mate of the tug *Admiral*, whom he had last seen drawn down to the waters of the North Sea. As the cry of one coming from the deep of death to claim justice upon the living were the words to him; and to the Spanish woman and her men they were as an inexplicable omen, which struck them with terror to their very marrows.

"Oh, Holy Mother! what is it? what does it mean? where does it come from?" she cried; and, as in answer to her, the wail rose again, with a long-drawn sob of "Ayo, ayo, ayo!" and then a horrid shriek of laughter, which was like a knife in the ear of those that heard it. Plaintive moaning and piercing cries followed upon the laughter, and were answered again by the shout of the burly voice below; but the unmistakably human note of this did nothing to reassure the Spaniards upon the ledge. Terror beyond control now seized upon them. Some cried aloud; others tried to turn their mules upon the path, and were with difficulty restrained; some fell into pious ejaculations; others, again, to deep and guttural curses. And while they stood, struck with apprehension of the unseen, lights began to move in the valley below them, soldiers came from the houses, the orders to fall in were heard in pure Spanish, horses were saddled quickly, and troops were soon perceived gathering in the single street of the solitary hamlet. The company, by a supreme ill-chance, had chosen for the passage of the ledge the very hour when a troop of mounted carabineers and a large body of infantry had bivouacked in the plain below it!

The appearance of the soldiers somewhat quelled the panic of the fugitives. It was clear after all that the enemy was man, and no ghostly apparition. No sooner were the troops visible beyond possibility of doubt than the woman shook her fears from her as leaves from a tree, and began to command again.

"Cowards!" she cried, with a curious forgetfulness of her own state five minutes gone, "cowards! will you let them shoot you as you ride? Where is your courage? Do you fear a handful of carabineers who are as dirt beneath your feet? I have shame for you."

But to Messenger she said—

"This is the moment. The second bridge is three hundred yards from here. Once past that, the danger is no more. But we must run the gauntlet, and some will fall. How light it is; a curse upon it! I never saw such a night."

"You didn't look to find men here—at least, you never mentioned it to me," said he, biting his lip in his perplexity.

"I did not look for the unexpected," she said in answer. "These men are returning, and not going; they have tired of the business yonder, and are getting home again. I could not foresee that. Their laziness has trapped us, and now they will shoot."

"If the light would only fail," said he next, "it would be as easy as walking along a road. I can't make it out; we seem to be focussed in the very centre of it. And what a light!"

She could not answer him, for as she turned about her startled exclamation was joined to his.

"Great God!" said he, "the wood is on fire!"

A deep lurid light glowed upon him as he spoke; it cast a crimson flush upon the darker shadows of the wood; it lit up the face of the precipice with an unsurpassable brilliancy. The fire kindled as a beacon on the hill-top by the friends of the Spanish woman had set flame to the surrounding thickets; and now from grass to grass, and bush to bush, and tree to tree, the devastation leapt with insatiable tongue. Even at the cramped station of the goat-track the company could follow its path— the path of radiant light and rolling smoke, and horrid roaring. It was as if some huge volcano had begun to vomit flames of wood, to wrap in its far-reaching light the stately pines, the coniferæ, the spreading chestnut, the climbing creepers. Now hissing, now crackling, now marking its way with the bursting asunder of rock and root, the fire crept on, bridging chasms, enveloping thickets, running swiftly to the summits of the loftiest trunks, sending the birds screaming and circling above it, driving the swine headlong into chasms and ravines, painting the sky with a quivering scarlet, beneath which the mighty clouds of smoke lay as hills and mountains raised magically in the ether.

Soon the hither valley was incarnadined; the troop of horsemen stood clear to be viewed as in the sun's light; the river shone as with red of blood; the flocks rushed wildly from pasture to pasture in unrestrained terror; the bells of the churches began to ring; the sleeping hamlets awoke. But those upon the ledge, for the most part dumb with their terror, could only rush on headlong towards the distant bridge, which would carry them from the amphitheatre of the hills; and, as they went, the fire crept slowly down to them, flakes of burning matter fell upon their mules, red-hot branches struck their faces, they were in danger of immediate suffocation from the vapour and the smoke which began to roll around them.

To the soldiers in the valley the spectacle was one for profound amazement. They had been sent to hunt down the English fugitives, but here was Nature doing the work. And they stood, dumb with astonishment, while the mules cried upon the path above, and the woman roared for the mule-men to press on, and the fire came down and yet down, so that at last it burnt upon the very edge of the goat-track, and men, and mules, and ponies began to fall headlong to the rocks below. And thus it stood that of the sixteen mules, seven had rolled into the valley, and there were but eight men left of the whole company when the small plateau which led to the ledge across the second chasm came in sight.

At this plateau a great ravine opened irregularly, having a breadth of thirty yards where the bridge was, but almost closing upon its summit, so that the fire, raging above, dropped burning flakes upon the woodwork of the bridge, and threatened every moment to consume it; while boughs and chunks of flaming wood and red-hot stones, and dying beasts were heaped pell-mell upon the open plain of rock which gave access to the passage.

To this semblance of shelter came at last the woman, and Messenger, and Fisher; but the nigger had gone over, and the number of mules was five, with but six men of the whole Spanish company. These now fell gasping upon the dangerous shelter of the plateau, and cried for the death which they felt must so surely come to them. But Messenger, almost falling from his pony, began to moan pitifully, and held to Fisher with a nervous grip which was eloquent of his fate. Fire had struck him in the face, and he was then quite blind.

"Hal!" he cried, as he clutched the strong hand held out to him, "I have lost my eyes! Hal, I'm blind, man, blind! my brain's burning! Let me have your hands! Oh, what darkness! my eyes are gone!"

"It can't be as bad as that, old man," cried Fisher, who held the extended hands with a firm grip. "Cling to me now, for we must cross the bridge. It won't last another ten minutes. Did you ever hear such a pandemonium as that old hag is making?"

"Where is she?" asked the other, holding to the lad with terrible desperation; "where are they all? Is the money safe? Don't you see that I'm in darkness? My brain's burning; I can't bear it; there's fire in my eyes now! Great Heaven, what pain!"

"The woman is now flogging the mule-men with her whip—at least, the five that are left," said Fisher. "They won't face the fire, and she's making them. Can't you hear her voice? But this is no place to stop, money or no money; the rocks are heating, and the bridge is beginning to burn."

"I'll stand by the woman, anyway," said Messenger,

suddenly drawing back; "we will sink or swim together. She's stood by me; and there's five hundred thousand pounds in it. Do you hear? I say the money's there; take me to it. I'll see it through. Where's Burke? And old Kenner. Halloa there, Kenner! Why don't you hail, man? You always were a tenderfoot, Kenner; you think on liquor. Ha! ha! drown your old carcase in it! Take me to the woman, lad; do you hear?"

Fisher, regardless of his delirium, quickly led him across the bridge, telling him that the way to the money lay there. It was a short passage, but the soldiers in the valley fired a volley vainly at them as they went; and the woodwork burned in places so fiercely that the soles of their feet were scorched. When they had come to the other side, the man dropped exhausted upon a grass bank; but the other stood up to watch the Spanish hag, who had compelled the muleteers now to venture upon the transit. She herself waited until the six men and the five beasts were treading the structure, before she rode boldly upon it, and, still commanding harshly, drove the terrified men forward towards the dangerous place where the fire burned most fiercely, and the wood was crackling briskly, as wood long dry and ready for the flame.

Had the bridge strength left to bear their passage? The question must have been put by a hundred men, who watched the transit from the valley below, for this was the supreme moment of the fire, when the

T

hills stood up with amazing clearness in the flood of light; and the valley of the rocks was red with a dazzling radiance as of the glow of jewels. The whole path of the burning in the wood now showed in a crimson field of ash of trees and grasses that shone red with the consuming heat. A few coverts—and these containing many great trees—yet burned about the chasm as torches, exceeding brilliant and fierce in their fires. The bridge itself was alight with flame; and men, both upon it and below it, heard themselves breathing in the moment of the peril.

It is just possible, had the Spaniards and the woman dared the passage on foot, that they had come to safety. The timidity of horse or mule in the face of fire is a fact as old as man; and it was the terror of the mules that ultimately brought the end of the venture. Although the arrieros had blindfolded the quaking brutes with strips torn from the shirts upon their backs, they were driven to the dangerous place only with a measure of extreme cruelty; and, so soon as the tongue of the flame was blown near to the first of them, the beast reared straight up, and fell back upon the one that followed him. A moment after, the pair of them, with their packs and riders, went bounding down to the crags of rock below, turning twice in the air as they went. Of the three behind, two endeavoured to wheel about upon the narrow planking, but broke away the balustrade, and fell quickly; but the last stood immovable, nor would whip nor words move him. Thus it came that the road was barred to the Spanish woman, who sat raving upon her pony, the light beating upon her as upon some beldame screeching; and, while she stood, the fire got firmer hold upon the bridge; and at last it broke, with a fountain of sparks and a rush of flame, and a great crash of blinding light: and beams and men and beasts went down to the darkness of the valley.

And this was the end of it, and of the man's hope; for, as the bridge fell, it took the woman with it in a sea of flame, and her cry of death rang out in the hills; but the cry was answered again by one far up in the heights, who wailed, as they had first heard him, a weird sobbing cry as of a doomed souL

CHAPTER XXVII.

IN THE VALLEY OF SILENCE.

It was early on the morning of the second day after the passage of the bridge when Fisher and Messenger began in any way to think of their future, or, for the matter of that, of escape from the place in which they found themselves. The crossing of the ravine had brought them to a great valley, which, for all the life in it, was a valley of silence, of dark woods and pools, and even of tiny cataracts where a river plunged from the higher mountains in its path to the sea. But impassable precipices shut them in on all sides; and, while this made for their protection from pursuit, the way of escape from the place of solitude was altogether hid from them.

To the lad the danger of the situation was plain from the beginning; but, though many hours had passed, the man was still in darkness. Blindness utter and hopeless, had come upon him, and he knew that never again would the veil be taken from his eyes. He could only lie upon the grass of a little wood to which the other had led him, and there shiver with his pain, scarce daring to ask, What has happened? where are the others? what is our situation? But Fisher tended him all through with hands as gentle as those of a loving woman. He bound his eyes with wet rags; he brought him abundantly of the luscious fruit that lay ripening everywhere around them; and he told him, in the best spirit of the consoler, that all would be well sooner or later.

This was sufficient for the moment, but soon it was evident that, if the man did not arouse himself before many hours passed, the two of them would die of sheer starvation where they lay. The nuts and the roots and the fruits were the poorest sustenance to men bruised in mind and in body; the shock of the terrible night compelled nature to call for strong remedies; and, though brandy was found in the bottle in Messenger's pocket, it was all insufficient for the more serious need. Thus it came that, after the man had slept for a few hours on the second night, Fisher spoke to him earnestly at dawn, and besought him to take heart for the journey.

"Look here," he said; "I'd sooner see you in the hands of the Spanish soldiers than lying in this state. At least they'd relieve your pain, and I can do nothing —nothing at all."

"What you could do you've done," said Messenger. "I should have died if it had not been for you. There's weight in my eyes enough to kill a man. I shall never see again!"

"Who can say that?" exclaimed Fisher earnestly. "Once we're back in civilisation, who knows what cannot be done for you? But, old man, we'll starve here."

"If it wasn't for you," said he, earnestly, "I'd cut my throat. What have I got to look to—years in a country I don't know, and me blind. Could anything be worse than that?"

"You say that now; but, when the danger's past, you'll think otherwise. You've always your head, Prince, and I can be your eyes."

"Ah!" said he, a sudden flush of a blind man's hope coming to him, "you'll be a friend to me now—now that I want it, Hal. And look, you're making me think again. If we could get on the road, I've money in my pocket. I filled up with sovereigns and ingots when the cases burst. I must hold at least a thousand pounds' worth of the stuff."

He pulled out, from the rags about his breast, a yellow bar of gold; and from the pockets of his trousers there came a handful of sovereigns, and then others, which he spread upon the turf and counted thrice.

"How much does it come to?" he asked, beginning to count again and feeling about for the gold with a wild touch. "Is it a hundred in all? I've been weighed down with it like a sack, but I brought it through. Hal, man, you won't cheat me now?"

"Cheat you!" cried Fisher, starting back. "Cheat *you*—God forbid!"

"Ah, I knew you wouldn't; but my head's going

with my eyes. You don't know what sight is to a man; but I'm learning. Give me the stuff again."

He gathered it all up to him, thrusting the ingot into the fold of his ragged shirt, while he counted the sovereigns with a wolf-like eagerness and mechanically tore the bandage from his eyes, revealing a forehead from which the flesh had gone; but his scorched and withered pupils stared into vacancy and gave him no light. Then he gnashed his teeth, and dug his hands into the grass, and foam came upon his lips.

"I will see, by Heaven!" he cried. "I'll have light—light, I tell you! Man, it's all dark—dark as death!"

His frenzy was the frenzy of the moment; but the paroxysm had robbed him of the money, which now rolled all around him, and he sat hugging his knees and chattering while Fisher bound up his head again with the rag damped in the river. Then the lad picked up the sovereigns from the grass and pressed them gently upon him.

"Here is your money," said he. "Had you not better put it back in your clothes?"

But the man had sobered down again.

"No," said he; "it's nothing to me; you hold to it. I was mad just now, and said things which you'll forget. Tell me, how did the woman go down?"

"She went down when the bridge burnt through; she was at the far end of it, and could not move either way. Didn't you hear her cry out?"

"Yes, I must have done. What a voice she had! Ha, ha! we should have made a pretty pair! So the hag knocked her brains out on the stones. Well, they were very good brains. I never met her like all the world through; she had the wits of ten men. What do you think she told me? That this place of hers was worth three thousand a year from the wrecks that came ashore alone. It seems that she and her people have lived here for years; it's a family place, and there never was one of them that didn't wreck. She was the last of her line; her husband, a Mexican, was shot in his own country a few years ago; but she must have lived a life! There's not a man within five miles that wasn't in league with her; and they brought the stuff from the ships into that lagoon of hers until they could sell it inland. That light we saw in the bay was a false light she put out to lure boats. Think of that in this day! Ah! it's enough to make you tingle, isn't it? and it was all her work!"

"I wonder they didn't fall foul of us when we came ashore," said Fisher, encouraging him to talk.

"So they would have done if we'd come in the daylight. The night saved us—and the rock. It wanted quick eyes to pick out the poop in the cradle if you didn't look for it; and, as you saw yourself, ships gave the reef a wide berth. That's nothing against the hag, for, once she heard of Englishmen being ashore, and her men got a glass on me, she put two and two together and made it four. If it hadn't been for the voice, we'd be half-way on the road to Finisterre, sure and safe. There was a curse in that cry; I said it when first I heard it."

"It was Billy, the mad boy, who called out," said Fisher thoughtfully; "he must have come off safe from the ship, and we never knew it."

"That's true,' said the other. "We'd never have found the nigger and the long-boat but for the firing. Well, it's all ended now, and we're adrift again. There was a curse upon it from the start."

"There must have been," was Fisher's answer.

"And now my eyes are burnt out, and you're going to say I brought it on me," said the man savagely. "You're ready with your tongue when there's that talk. If ever I come to decent land again, I'll put a white tie on you and send you out to croak. You'd make a fortune giving the old women their sherry; you're just the build. But give me men, I say, and curse all twaddle!"

Fisher let him talk, for this was his mood. Presently he came to quiet again, and said—

"Where are we now? What's the place like?"

"It seems to me to be a forest between the hills," said Fisher. "There's a wood to your left, and a great stretch of grassland in front of us. But, for all the way I see out, we might be in a basin."

"There must be a road," said the man impatiently, "or the woman wouldn't have come here. What's that singing noise I hear?—it's falling water, isn't it?"

"I went that way last night," said Fisher; "there is a river, but it rushes down like a cataract."

"Then follow it," said the Prince, "follow it through. The road should lie where it breaches the hills. That's sense, isn't it? I'm strong enough now; and dark here or dark there, what's the odds?"

"I think you're right," exclaimed Fisher, who had become timid before the other's brusqueness; "but, Prince, you're very bitter with me."

"Bitter," said the man, who had stood up at his words; "bitter with you? No, not that; you stand between me and death. Let me hold your hands—let me hold them tight. I've no eyes, and the darkness presses down upon me; you'll be my eyes now. Heaven knows, you're the only one in my life that I ever cared to see twice—man, I just loved you."

"Then we'll face it together," said the other, "if you'll have me for a friend, Prince."

The Prince laughed at the suggestion.

"Hal," said he, "it looks as if I had no choice— I must just put up with you. Let me lean upon your arm. I feel as if I were going down-hill; the ground sinks away from me wherever I put my feet. I'll be better when I've walked a spell. What's the road like in front?"

"There's a dingle full of long grass and a mass of flowers. The place is as wild as a jungle, and almost dark with the shadow of the trees."

"Are you sure there's no one in sight?"

"Not a living soul."

"Well, I'm keen of hearing, and I think you're right; but there'll be work to do when we get out into the open. You won't forget that they'll watch the road like a trap; and I don't see what's to prevent us being taken."

"We shall die here, anyway," said Fisher; "we may as well face it, if it's only on the odd chance."

They had come into the depths of the thicket, and their boots were dyed with the gold of the flowers upon which they trod. Long marsh grass, from which sprang orchids and ox-eyes and ivies abundantly, led them down a silent avenue, where birds of rich plumage rose up, startled at their coming; and a myriad flies buzzed ceaselessly about them. Then they struck the river where it narrowed until it became a stream not fifteen yards wide, scouring between rugged banks of white earth towards the lower end of the silent valley.

At a break in the banks of this swiftly-flowing stream they lay down to quench their thirst, and when the man's eyes had been again bound up in the wetted rag, he threw himself upon the ground as he was wont to do in the old time, and listened for the sound of men moving or of voices. When he had satisfied himself that no such sounds were to be heard, he rose up more cheerfully, and prepared to continue the journey.

"It's clear," he said, as the pair of them tramped

along briskly in spite of their fatigue, "that the woman used this river as her road out of the hills; and we must use it, too. How, I can't tell you now, but the way will show presently."

Fisher thought so too, but he only said "Yes," for anxiety was pressing upon him, and weariness and hunger. He thought often that he could not drag his weary limbs another step, and he walked mechanically for nearly an hour, while the stream alternately ran between high banks of rock or spread itself abroad in the valley, broadening until it swept the long grasses and the lilies, and washed the leaves of the overhanging trees. At last, however, and when the exhausted men had come under the very shadow of the great hill which stood as a barrier between them and the outer world, it narrowed again, running between high ramparts of rock straight towards the headland.

Some time before the two had reached this place, Fisher had uttered an exclamation whose dominant note was one of surprise but to the man's quick inquiry, "What is it?" he made no answer, only hurrying him on. When he stopped ultimately, it was upon the border of a pool, in which the water swirled fiercely before it entered the cutting; and in this pool a rude punt, almost round in shape, was moored. There was only a pole in the ship, and a big locker at one end of it; but it was, beyond doubt, the last resort of the woman, and the means between herself and secret flight from the castle. The sight of it was as wine to the lad.

"Prince!" he cried, with delight, "you've eyes now for ten of us! Here's what you were looking for —a punt against the bank, and a pole in it."

"I was expecting it half an hour ago," said Messenger. "Well, we'll just get in, and leave the rest to chance. Is the river swift?"

"It runs like a mill."

"All the better; where the woman went we may go. Just place me where I can hold tight, and keep her in the centre of the stream. If there's going to be any shooting, I prefer to be on my back.'

He was guided in, and set comfortably, with his back against the locker, almost as he spoke; and then Fisher rolled up his sleeves and cast free the mooring. A gentle push drove the punt from the bank, but the stream caught it as a match, and sent it whirling wildly round, with the spray foaming over it, and the water wetting the two to their skins.

At one time, Fisher declared that their venture would end where it began; but he had seen something of river work, and, when he had recovered himself from the first shock, he contrived to get a hold for his pole, and sent the rickety craft rocking into the deep of the stream. It was carried thence swiftly between the high banks; and from that moment the peril of the journey began.

Of this, Messenger himself knew nothing. He experienced only the sensation of swift travel through the air; he heard the harsh grating when the tub struck the bank, or bounded off the embossment of a jutting rock; he was conscious that his companion was in the throes of ceaseless work and activity. But to Fisher the picture was very different. Though the heavy wooden tub was abnormally strong, he thought every moment to see her crushed into splinters as the rapids drove her onwards at a headlong pace, and the river-bed inclined until the stream itself was like a roaring torrent.

As the craft thus was forced onward, the banks upon either side of the river became higher, until it seemed as if the punt were being carried into the very bowels of the earth. Deep and dark and infinitely green the torrent ran in its rocky bed, sinking and yet sinking until it fell, as it were, under the shadow of the hill; and all that could be seen from the boat were precipices of stone, and great heights which no man could ascend. But yet its course was straight as the rule upon the line, and the ship kept from wreckage upon the bank with the least touch of the skilfully-handled pole. Then, quickly, the light in the abyss failed; a tremendous roaring, as of a mighty cascade, rang in the ears of the two; they were plunged into utter darkness, and the cries died upon their lips as the punt bounded onwards with shocks innumerable, and great crashes, and the sound of wood splintering.

The truth was that they had entered a tunnel, cut by Nature, under the great hill which was one of the ramparts of the valley; and they now voyaged through the bowels of the earth. Fisher, indeed, had

"THE RAPIDS DROVE HER ONWARDS AT A HEADLONG PACE" (*p*. 318).

seen the orifice of the subterranean way long before he had reached it, but had waited until they were near to the approach before he had called to Messenger to throw himself flat, and, on his part, had hauled in his pole and lain down, holding to the crossplanks with all his strength. From that time, both the nature of the passage and the manner of it were hidden from him. He could tell little beyond the terror of the transit when, in the darkness, he felt the boat spinning round and round like a top; or striking the rock with fearful concussion; or flying downwards like a ship upon the fall of a sea. And he wondered that the punt held together, that she was not shivered like a glass falling upon stone, that he did not feel the water about his ears and mouth, and come to the unutterable struggle for life and breath in that tomb of horror and of noise.

All this went through his mind like a dream, for the duration of the passage was brief. When it seemed that he could endure the thunderous echoing in his ears no longer, when the crashing of the boat was most violent, when the water poured over him in a cascade, light flashed upon his eyes, a brown burnt landscape spread out before him, he saw a thicket with a green bank of grass before it, a village lying in a hollow upon his right hand, a distant view of purple hills and white misted sky. And at this he stood up again and grasped his pole, as the punt was swung gently through meadow-land.

"Prince," he cried, joyfully, "we're through it now: here's the open country again."

"What do you see?" asked the man, sitting up.

"A great stretch of burnt meadow-land, and a wood upon the left bank—but halloa!"

"Well——?"

"There are two soldiers lying by the river!"

CHAPTER XXVIII.

THE HARBOUR OF THE POOL.

THE punt was now travelling so swiftly that the lad had scarce time to throw himself down before the whole of the danger was apparent. The two infantrymen were lying upon a bank of grass at the border of a thicket; their rifles were resting against the trunk of a chestnut-tree; there were the embers of a fire smouldering; a couple of empty wine-bottles had rolled from the place of picnic to the very edge of the stream; but the men themselves were fast in sleep, their heads covered with their forage-caps, and their sandals showing in the grass as the shoes of men who lie flat upon their backs in the enjoyment of unbroken rest.

"Prince," said Fisher, when he had looked long, "there are only two of them, and they're sleeping!"

"Are you sure of that?" whispered Messenger.

"There's no doubt of it. I can see their feet sticking up in the grass, and they've pulled their caps over their eyes."

"Then set the boat in the straight, and drop when you're near enough. If she's in the middle of the

U

stream, she should go down easy. What's the river here?"

"Twenty yards, and thick with rushes," replied Fisher; "but the current's huge."

"All the better; we'll go the faster!"

He said no more, but waited expectantly while Fisher kept the craft off the reeds, and let her go swinging down the very centre of the waterway. They were now within fifty yards of the sentries; but still the sleepers lay motionless, the flies buzzing about their ears, the shade deep upon their faces. Would they wake? The lad's brain was on fire as he asked the question.

At the very foot of the thicket's bank, bush and bramble flourished, spreading upon the water. The river here ran almost at a level with the meadows, but was thick with weeds at its shallow sides; and, when the punt came quite to the place where the sentries lay, she touched the long grasses and ground over them with a sound of scraping which made the two within her shiver as men struck with cold. So loud was the noise of her passage that one of the sentries turned in his sleep, and then sat up on his hams dreamily. Had it not been for the thick bush which lay between the stream and his camping-place, the voyage would have ended upon the spot; but it chanced that the tangle of weeds held the punt momentarily still; the noise ceased; the man saw nothing; he kicked his companion, swore at him, drank something from a bottle, and composed himself to sleep again. Then Fisher, who lay in the prow like a cat, used his arms with silent strength, and thrust the unwieldy tub again into the stream, where she was caught quickly, and whirled onwards, through the meadows of maize, to the heart of the great valley below the mountains.

For another hour the weary men endured the confinement of the punt and the full heat of the unclouded sun. They said little to one another, for the reaction of the excitement was strong upon them; nor did they see a single soldier, or pass any other village, until they were three or four miles from the first coming-out of the tunnel. But, an hour after noon, they entered a great pool, which Fisher called a glade of the waters—a pool arched over with poplars and tropic-like leaves, and bordered with ripe green banks, which were almost hid by the blue and the scarlet and the yellow of innumerable flowers. So seductive was the haven, so full of dreamy silence, so alluring to one who could scarce stand for fatigue, that Fisher brought the punt against its banks, and, not daring to tell all its delights to a man who could see none of them, he said—

"There's a fine place to land, if you think it's time."

"It's time enough, if the place is right," said the man. "What will there be on the banks here?"

"There's an open wood to your left hand, and a thicket upon the far shore. From what I can see of it, a road should pass near the trees here."

"Let's get out, then. I shall die of cramp if I lie here another hour; but you'll have to set my feet on the banks; and you won't be leaving me—to reconnoitre or anything like that?"

"I'll not leave you a minute," said Fisher; "it's my promise."

The man mumbled something and took the hand stretched out to him. His fear of solitude was, both then and for months afterwards, one of the most curious symptoms of his affliction. The dark in which henceforth he was to live so acted upon his nerves that he could hardly compel himself to let Fisher leave him even for the space of a minute. He slept with his companion's arm near to his; and now, when he had come ashore, and lay down upon the soft grass, he had no rest until the lad took one of his hands and held it. And so, with their heads pillowed upon the grass, and the shade of the willows to give them cool, the two, worn and weary, and very near to tears, slept through the heat of the day, and until the angelus was ringing in the villages.

CHAPTER XXIX.

MATTERS OF HISTORY.

IN looking back upon the many scenes which I have been able to set about the tragedy of Arnold Messenger and his associates, I mind me that I have spoken little—nor was other course possible—of the English and the European view of this most daring emprise, and of the means which the authorities in many countries took to combat it. Yet, for the fuller understanding of the ultimate issue, and for the realisation of many things now lying in mystery, it is necessary that something should be said upon pages well back in the record, and upon certain episodes which are but mentioned in the writing.

For these things, English newspapers are my clearest authority, and I find in them a very exact account of much that I have dealt with, and of other matters about which Messenger himself had no complete knowledge. He, on his part, was not able, until he met the Spanish woman, to understand how pursuit first came upon him; wanting the information simply because he did not know that the Irish mate of the tug *Admiral* was picked up, with Conyers, whom he had freed, by the steamer that loomed upon the horizon at the very moment the little vessel cocked her stern above the North Sea. Had this been plain to him, he would have anticipated the sequence. The two men, being carried by the steamer to Bergen, wired thence news of the deed to London; and the whole city was stirred almost as by the story of a war.

To Capel, Martingale & Co., the tidings came as a blow which shook the house to its foundations. The head himself, shamed at the fall of his nephew, Sydney Capel, was henceforth little else but a broken man whose wits were gone. But his partners worked like slaves to help the underwriters and to avert their loss. All the vast influence of the great firm and of Lloyds was brought to bear upon Governments and upon police. Skilled detectives left for Lisbon, for Paris, for Monte-Video. Cruisers were sent to scour the North Sea, the common belief being that Kenner's yacht was running for Holland or for Norway; other cruisers searched the channel; others, again, the coast of Ireland, though these were few, since no man seems to have anticipated the yacht's flight round the capes of Scotland.

How it came about that the *Nero* sighted the *Semiramis* and pursued her, I have already told; but the curious cessation of the pursuit at the moment of its seeming triumph is a mystery with the simplest solution. The vessel broke her screw-shaft when she was within an ace of victory. The huge mass of metal, rioting in the aft-cabins, split skin and plates until the miracle stood that the ship continued to float. She was brought to Bordeaux with the utmost difficulty, and thence she sent home news of her work, though that was known already at the Admiralty; and other cruisers searched the French coast and the northern shore of Spain. It was one of these, as we have seen, which anchored ultimately in the very bay where the fugitives were harboured; and although its men came at length upon the wreckage in the cradle of the reef, they did not do so until the money was ashore, and the Englishmen were hid in the shelter of the castle.

From this moment the scent was, as goes the schoolboy saying, hot to excitement. The authorities in London waited to hear every day of the capture of the bullion and of the missing crew. Capel, Martingale & Co., who had recently negotiated a Spanish loan, brought pressure to bear at Madrid; and companies of soldiers were sent up from Vivero and Finisterre. With each of these there was an English detective, and for the better purposes of identification no less an agent than Mike Brennan, the former mate of the *Admiral*, was sent with the company of infantry which watched the burning of the bridge. He it was who had heard the daft lad Billy calling in the hills; and he had recognised the voice and answered the cry, to the fear and panic of the doomed muleteers.

When the end of the venture came, it was the general impression amongst the Spanish soldiers that all, with the woman, had perished in the great fire, which is talked of to-day in hushed whispers by the peasantry; and will be tradition to their children's children. But, as there was a possibility that Messenger had escaped, the search was continued for some weeks. The chasm was bridged again; sentries were posted about the whole amphitheatre of hills; the silent valley was searched from end to end; and the matter ended by the officer in charge of the troops sending to Madrid his emphatic opinion that the Englishmen never crossed the bridge, since there was no way of escape over the ramparts of the valley for man or for beast. The supposition that there was a possible passage through the tunnel never entered his head. Doggedly he formed an opinion, as Spaniards do, and no human argument would have turned him from it.

Thus it happened that London heaved a sigh of disappointment in the belief that a prince of rogues would not figure in her Law Courts, and began to ask, What of the money? And it was consoled as, almost ingot by ingot, the bullion was restored to the firm from whom it had been stolen. Some of it was found in the inner lagoon of the woman's house; much in the valley below the goat-track, where the peril of the flight had begun; and the remaining cases—or rather their contents, for the cases were shivered to splinters—in the ravine and amongst the embers of the fallen bridge. When the amount thus regained was estimated at its value, the firm considered themselves the losers of two hundred and fifty thousand pounds. Of this sum, a great part had been pillaged by the Spanish soldiers; the servants of the woman had not neglected to snap up what they could; Messenger had a fraction; the peasantry slyly pocketed many a sovereign, and continued for the best part of a year after the tragedy to spend their leisure in the valley of the disaster turning logs and cutting grasses in the hope that gold would be found. But the soldiers were sent to their quarters in the month following the supreme disaster; and they went willingly, as men who had accomplished a great work, and must recreate long, lest their strength should fail them or their energy become chronic.

CHAPTER XXX.

THE END OF THE RECORD.

WHEN Fisher awoke by the banks of the silent pool, it was with a start and an exclamation upon his lips. A hand had touched him gently upon the shoulder, and he sprang to his feet, thinking that the soldiers had entrapped him while he slept. But he met the gaze only of a white-haired old man, whose cassock and bands proclaimed him to be a priest; and he heard a gentle voice speaking quickly in bad French.

"Ne vous dérangez pas," cried the old fellow, as he put his hand upon the lad's shoulder; "et taisez vous. I did know Madame—sans doute; sans doute." And then, with an attempt, exceedingly poor, to speak English, he continued: "Trust upon me, I come for friend—the soldiers, ah, no good, no good, no good!" and he shook his head as though the conviction was painful to him.

Messenger had started up at the first word he spoke; and when he found that Fisher was not near him his distress was uncontrollable. He shouted loudly, with a very bitter cry; and when the lad ran up to him, he began to ask many questions at a breath.

"Why do you leave me?" said he savagely; "you know I can't move a hand. Who were you talking to? I heard another voice."

At this, the old priest spoke for himself, much as he had done to Fisher; but he gave a cry when he saw that the man was blind, and gabbled sympathy in Spanish. To this, Messenger answered in French, asking—

"Why have you come here; is it to help us?"

"I heard of the trouble at the castle, and of the presence of Englishmen there," said the priest, speaking in the same tongue. "Madame was very kind to me. Her friends are my friends. An hour ago one of my people saw you sleeping here, and came running to my house. And I am here. Consider me your servant as I was hers."

"We want food and rest, and shelter from these sharks in sandals," said Messenger, none too pleasantly; "will you give us that?"

"I will do to you as I would to a son," cried the old man; "I am the servant of God and the brother of the outcast; if you trust me, you shall come out of Spain. If you stay here, the troopers will pass in a few hours, and you will go to Madrid with them. The choice must be yours. What I do is done for Madame. I have lost a great friend; no man had a greater. She was such a woman as we shall not see again, my children. God rest her soul!"

Messenger heard the tale through, and bit his nails.

"What's he like to look at?" he asked Fisher in a whisper; "can you read him at all?"

"He seems to me to be about eighty, and has the whitest hair I ever saw. It's a face to trust. And we've no choice that I see," said he again, as the other still thought upon it. "We'll be taken here for a certainty before noon to-morrow."

"Very well; that seems sense, and we may as well face this risk as another. But keep your eyes open, and call out if you see anything. I'm just dying for want of food."

With this he turned to the old man who had appeared in their path so strangely, and he answered with less of brusqueness.

"We accept your offer," said he, "and put our lives in your hands. When you give them back to us, we shall find means to thank you substantially. If, on the other hand, you have come here with a tale, we shall be equally ready in settling the account. We are both near gone for want of food and drink, and we'll thank you to hurry."

"As I do to you, so may God do to me," said the old man with fervent benevolence; and, at that, he tucked his skirts about his legs, and set a brisk pace down the woodland path. A very short walk brought them to the head of the thicket; but the priest kept the shelter of its outskirts for some ten minutes before he struck across a marshy meadow, and came upon the back of a village which was almost hid in a clump of chestnuts. His own house was not a road's breadth from the little spire which stuck up amongst the green of the trees; and when he entered it, he did so by the garden, bringing the men ultimately to his sitting-room without observance from anyone. But he showed them at the window of the apartment how much they owed to him. A company of lancers was about the door of the *venta*; and, at a later hour, carabineers passed through the village on the road to Ferrol.

In this old priest's house the fugitives were sheltered for three weeks, receiving from him a simple hospitality and a large sympathy. At the end of the second week, there was brought to them the girl Inez, who looked to this old man alone for shelter, and who was being sent by him to a convent at Cadiz. The child had many hours of better happiness than she had ever known as she walked with Fisher in the high-walled garden near the church; and while in the spell of her company, and telling her that their hope could lie only in a future which should begin after years had sped, the lad built up the purpose of his life, it was yet his greatest bitterness that friendship must drive him alike from her and from civilisation. And she, clinging to him as to one drawn suddenly from the outer world to befriend her, urged upon him the claim of the blind man; and even with her kisses upon his lips, he held himself straight in the difficult paths he had chosen.

Thus weeks of a delicious happiness passed all too quickly; and when the time was ripe, Hal, brushing away with his lips the childish tears which fell abundantly, went with the priest and Messenger; and the two being disguised as Spanish peasants, they came safely to Vigo, where the influence of the ecclesiastic and his money procured them passage to Monte-Video.

In that city I met them, two months after they had landed; and there had this story from them, as I have set it out. The man was still blind; the lad waited on him like a brother.

"I could not leave him now," said he. "He has no eyes but mine."

Yet no writing could convey the note of pity in his voice as he spoke the words.

THE END.

www.ingramcontent.com/pod-product-compliance
Lightning Source LLC
Chambersburg PA
CBHW030315240426
43673CB00040B/1173